Are there different types of ADHD?

What can I do to help the doctor make an accurate diagnosis?

If my child is being evaluated for ADHD, what questions should I ask?

If ADHD can't be cured, what are the goals of treatment?

Besides medication, what other treatments are used for ADHD?

Should my child be in psychotherapy?

What kind of side effects can I expect to see from the various medications?

What should I do if my child gets the wrong dose?

What steps should the teacher and school take to help my child succeed in the classroom?

You'll discover the answers to these questions and hundreds more in . . .

THE ATTENTION DEFICIT ANSWER BOOK

ALAN WACHTEL, M.D., is clinical associate professor of psychiatry at New York University's School of Medicine and a fellow of the American Psychiatric Association. He is the founder and director of Familyhealth Associates, a private practice specializing in the diagnosis and treatment of attenti behavior, and learning disorders, with offices and White Plains, New York. He lectur learning disorders throughout th the New York metropolitan area

MICHAEL BOYETTE is a veteran and the author of seven health books, inclu _oung the Melatonin Way_ (Plume), which he wrote with St en Bock, M.D. He lives with his family in Philadelphia.

THE
ATTENTION DEFICIT ANSWER BOOK

THE BEST MEDICATIONS AND PARENTING STRATEGIES FOR YOUR CHILD

Alan Wachtel, M.D.
with Michael Boyette

A LYNN SONBERG BOOK

PLUME

Readers should bear in mind that this book is not intended to be used for self-diagnosis or self-treatment and that they should consult their doctors about any and all medical problems. Research about attention deficit disorder is ongoing and subject to interpretation. Although all reasonable efforts have been made to include the most up-to-date and accurate information in this book, there can be no guarantee that what we know about this complex subject won't change with time. Further, research about prescription drugs is an ongoing process; side effects and adverse reactions to particular drugs sometimes continue to be reported to the FDA after a drug has been approved for use in the general market. Readers should never stop taking a prescription drug or alter the dosage or dosing schedule without first consulting their physicians. The publisher, the authors, and the producer disclaim all responsibility for any possible consequences from any treatment, action, or application of medicine by any person reading or following the information in this book.

PLUME
Published by the Penguin Group
Penguin Putnam Inc., 375 Hudson Street,
New York, New York 10014, U.S.A.
Penguin Books Ltd, 27 Wrights Lane,
London W8 5TZ, England
Penguin Books Australia Ltd, Ringwood,
Victoria, Australia
Penguin Books Canada Ltd, 10 Alcorn Avenue,
Toronto, Ontario, Canada M4V 3B2
Penguin Books (N.Z.) Ltd, 182–190 Wairau Road,
Auckland 10, New Zealand

Penguin Books Ltd, Registered Offices:
Harmondsworth, Middlesex, England

First published by Plume, an imprint of Dutton Signet, a member
of Penguin Putnam Inc.

First Printing, January, 1998
10 9 8 7 6 5 4 3

LIBRARY OF CONGRESS CATALOGING-IN-PUBLICATION DATA:
Wachtel, Alan, M.D.
    The attention deficit answer book : the best medications and parenting strategies for your child / Alan Wachtel with Michael Boyette.
        p. cm.
    "A Lynn Sonberg book."
    Includes index.
    ISBN 0-452-27941-0
    1. Attention-deficit-disordered children–Rehabilitation. 2. Parenting. I. Boyette, Michael. II. Title.
    RJ506.H9W32   1998
    618.92'8589–dc21   97-13422
                                                                         CIP

Printed in the United States of America
Set in New Baskerville
Designed by Leonard Telesca

Contents

CHAPTER 1

A Complex Condition

If you're reading this book, chances are that you or someone you love has been diagnosed with attention deficit hyperactivity disorder—ADHD for short.

It is also likely that your doctor recommended Ritalin as the "preferred" treatment option.

But naturally, you have some questions. What is this strange and perplexing thing called ADHD? Sure, you may say, my child is having some problems, but is he truly "sick"—or just obstinate? Does she really need this medication?* Will it work? And is it safe?

In this book, we'll examine the questions that parents—as well as doctors and other health care practitioners—ask about Ritalin and other drugs used to treat ADHD. No doubt your doctor has given you the broad outlines of the disorder and treatment options. But ADHD and its treatment are far more complex than they might seem at first. In addition, new research is rapidly changing the way we think about the dis-

---

*In the past, ADHD was widely regarded as a "boys only" condition, but more recent research shows that it's also common among girls. To acknowledge that fact, I've alternated the use of male and female pronouns when referring to ADHD patients throughout the book.

order. For example, some of the time-honored ideas about ADHD—that it's mostly a disorder of boys, that it gets better all by itself, that it causes behavior problems—are turning out not to be true after all.

Similarly, new research is changing the way we think about treatment. It turns out that traditional ADHD drugs—Ritalin included—and dosage regimens aren't necessarily the best option for many people. In fact, when treatment fails, it's usually because all of the options haven't been fully explored and tailored to the patient's individual needs.

❐ More than Meets the Eye

First, you should know that ADHD isn't just a fancy name for bad behavior. It's a medical condition involving the way information is processed in the brain. Sophisticated studies show actual differences in brain chemistry between people with ADHD and people without it.

Traditionally, three components—*attention, impulsiveness,* and *hyperactivity*—formed the classic picture of children with ADHD. These were the kids who had trouble establishing and, especially, maintaining attention; who couldn't control impulses (for example, blurting out answers in class); and who showed an excessive level of physical activity.

More recently, however, we've come to realize that many cases of ADHD don't fit this classic profile. Not every child with ADHD tears up the classroom or darts into the street. Some are quiet, well-behaved, soft-spoken people.

The common thread, however, is the attentional problem. Every child with ADHD has difficulty focusing on things. They're distractible. They lose things. They're absentminded. If you send them upstairs to get their shoes, you'll find them twenty minutes later looking at a comic book.

In the majority of cases, medication controls the symptoms of ADHD and allows people with the condition to lead normal and fulfilling lives. And more than forty years of experience, both in the lab and in doctors' offices, show that medication is both safe and effective.

But that's not the end of the story. Because there's more to ADHD than meets the eye.

Take diagnosis, for example. You can't treat effectively until you've made an accurate diagnosis. But there's no simple test for ADHD—no culture, no blood test, no eye chart that will clinch the diagnosis. And there are many conditions that mimic the symptoms of ADHD, ranging from drug abuse to anxiety to depression to lead poisoning.

Even though the symptoms look similar, the treatments for these conditions are radically different. So unless your doctor makes the proper diagnosis and rules out "mimickers," she may end up treating the wrong disorder and wondering why the treatment doesn't work. Or you may have the problem in reverse—your child may be under treatment for depression, anxiety, or another condition when he or she really has ADHD.

Even with proper diagnosis, you're not out of the woods. Treatment of ADHD can be complicated too. Is Ritalin the best medication option? Not always. And is medication enough? No.

ADHD doesn't occur in a vacuum; it affects—and is affected by—everything else in life. Medication may control the symptoms of ADHD, but it doesn't treat the strain that families feel in coping with the consequences of ADHD. It may help a child do better in school, but it can't transform the classroom into an environment that supports the needs of children with ADHD and helps them succeed. And it can make someone more attentive, but it can't undo the years of struggle and frustration that people suffer before their condition is identified and treated. In this book, I hope to offer some guidance on how to confront and resolve these deeper issues.

The good news is that ADHD, properly diagnosed and

treated, is an extremely manageable disorder. We cannot cure it, and contrary to earlier beliefs it doesn't go away on its own. But we have the tools—not only medication, but also behavioral techniques, psychological interventions, school modifications, and the like—that can help people with ADHD. As we have learned more about how to identify and treat this complex and mysterious condition, we have been able to offer countless people the ability to lead happy, productive, and fulfilled lives. It is one of modern medicine's best success stories.

My goal in this book is to help you understand these complexities and, working with your own physician, come up with the best treatment approach possible. Because of its complexities, ADHD isn't a problem that doctors can treat on their own. It requires an informed partnership among you, your child, teachers, and family, as well as the physician.

Your child's pediatrician may be seeing dozens of children with ADHD, each for only a few minutes every few weeks. You, however, know your child better than anyone, and you're in the best position to get what he or she needs.

For example, most pediatricians don't have enough time to delve into the social adjustment issues, such as difficulties in making friends, that your child may face as a result of ADHD. So it's important for you, as a parent, to be aware that such issues exist and to know how they should be addressed. Similarly, your child's school may not be aware of all the techniques they can use to enhance the classroom environment for children with ADHD—and it often falls to enlightened parents to bring this information to the school's attention.

Also, because ADHD is such a multifaceted disorder, it's difficult for any one professional to have the whole picture. A pediatrician tends to focus on how it's treated; a teacher on how it affects learning, and so on. It's often left to parents to bring these varying perspectives together into one comprehensive plan.

By answering some of the questions that parents have

brought to me over the years, I hope to give you the information you need to make this partnership work. The book is organized in a question-and-answer format, highlighting typical concerns that parents face as they confront the issues of ADHD. In addition, the chapters reflect the various stages that parents and children face as they go from the earliest signs of ADHD through childhood and adolescence and into adulthood. Each stage brings its own issues and concerns.

You will find in this book an emphasis on medical treatments. We'll talk about medications that may be better alternatives to Ritalin for your child, medications that can be used in combination with Ritalin, and ways to make Ritalin more effective.

We'll also look at nondrug approaches to managing ADHD, including scientific evidence showing that these approaches must be used *with*, not *instead of* medication. Parents' concerns about medication are understandable, and doctors must make every effort to use the lowest possible doses that will control the symptoms. Through careful diagnosis, physicians must make sure that these drugs are used only in cases where they're indicated. And through ongoing monitoring, they must make sure that medications are doing what they're supposed to, with the fewest possible side effects.

CHAPTER 2

Getting an Accurate Diagnosis

Probably the single most common reason that Ritalin and other ADHD treatments fail is because they're being used to treat the wrong disorder.

To use these medications effectively, you have to begin with an accurate diagnosis. And yet this is often the most difficult part of the treatment program to get right. Often, what appears to be ADHD turns out to be something quite different—for example, depression or anxiety. By the same token, ADHD can masquerade for a lifetime as something else—forgetfulness, laziness, even senility.

With ADHD, there's no laboratory test or specific clinical finding that can clinch the diagnosis. In most cases, the doctor can't even rely on his own observations alone; he must sift through the patient's history, the reports of family members, teachers and counselors, and the patient's own experiences.

Though other conditions may look similar to ADHD, their treatments are quite different—and definitely not interchangeable with that for ADHD. Not only does the condition not get better, but the patient is needlessly exposed to medications she doesn't need. And perhaps worst of all, treatment failures that occur because of misdiagnosis cause patients and their families to lose faith. They assume they belong to that small category of patients for whom treatments are not effective. Or they conclude that they've been betrayed—that the promised benefits of treatment don't really exist—and lose hope.

❑ How Is ADHD Diagnosed?

The condition is diagnosed through a combination of the doctor's own observations; the evaluations of parents, teachers, and counselors; and the patient's history. There are a number of educational and neuropsychological tests that can *help* make the diagnosis, but there's no single test that can tell you whether someone has ADHD.

The most commonly accepted diagnostic criteria for ADHD are defined in the DSM-IV—the official diagnostic manual of the American Psychological Association. These criteria boil down to three key areas: attention, impulsivity, and hyperactivity.

Attention: The person with ADHD has trouble maintaining *sustained* attention and focus for any long period of time. With conscious effort, the ADHD child can maintain focus, but it's difficult and can't be sustained. Attention can also be maintained when the environment is especially stimulating (e.g., video games and action pictures).

Some parents tell me their child can't have ADHD because "she can pay attention when she wants to." That doesn't mean she doesn't have ADHD. For anyone, whether they have the disorder or not, the ability to maintain focus varies depending on countless factors: The degree of interest or fear, other distractions, time of day, fatigue, hunger—the list goes on and on. And in some situations, a child with ADHD has absolutely no problem paying attention.

What makes these children different is that they can't sustain attention in situations where others can. For example, few kids like to do math homework. But most can do it and stay on task. ADHD kids can't. That's when you see the differences.

Impulsivity: This symptom is usually but not always present in ADHD. It involves the inability to control or moderate impulses, and it can involve a wide range of behaviors: excessive motor activity, speaking out of turn, rushing through tasks, and so on. A child who's impulsive doesn't look before she leaps—literally and figuratively. She'll blurt out the answer instead of raising her hand. She'll chase a ball into the street. She can't keep a secret. Interestingly, we find these children also tend to jump the gun on tasks involving very basic motor skills—for example, if they're asked to press a key whenever a certain letter appears on a computer screen, they're more likely to press the key before they're sure what the letter is.

These findings suggest that impulsiveness isn't just a personality trait; it's a fundamental physical characteristic of a person's nervous system.

Hyperactivity: Like impulsivity, hyperactivity is sometimes but not always present in ADHD. It's more than just a high energy level; it's a high level of inappropriate activity. Like impulsivity, hyperactivity implies difficulty controlling certain behaviors and activities. Often with these children, we see at least one body part in motion at all times. If they're drumming their fingers and we ask them to stop, the foot starts tapping. If we call attention to their foot, they'll stop—but then their head starts bobbing up and down.

What do these three components have in common?

On a physical level, they all involve activity in the frontal lobes of the brain. Behaviorally, they seem to be interrelated as well. For example, you can think of hyperactivity as a kind of physical corollary of impulsiveness. And both inattentiveness and impulsiveness involve problems of self-control and focus.

This issue of control is the common thread in ADHD

symptoms. People with ADHD have difficulty controlling what they pay attention to and when. They have trouble controlling impulses. And they have trouble controlling their activity levels.

Are there different types of ADHD?

ADHD *always* involves attentional problems. But it can occur with or without impulsiveness, and with or without hyperactivity. As we'll see later on, these variations may affect which medications are used for treatment.

One of the biggest changes in the latest revision of the DSM criteria is an increased emphasis on the difference between the *inattentive* type of ADHD and the *hyperactive* type. We've come to realize that many, many cases of ADHD don't involve hyperactivity. And we recognize, too, that the greater risks come from inattention, not from hyperactivity, because kids who can't pay attention have trouble learning.

What other conditions might cause problems with attention, impulse control, or hyperactivity?

There are many kinds of medical problems that can resemble certain features of ADHD. It's important to rule these out for three reasons: (1) The treatments used for ADHD generally aren't effective for these conditions; (2) misguided treatment exposes your child to medication unnecessarily; and (3) the wrong diagnosis will delay appropriate treatment for the *real* problem.

Here are the most common of these "mimickers":

Everyday problems can mimic ADHD. For example: Is your child getting enough sleep at night? (Fatigue will cause inattention.) If your child tends to be unfocused and disruptive just before lunchtime, maybe he or she is simply hungry.

Learning disabilities (LDs) such as dyslexia can mimic ADHD—especially in their effects on academic performance. It's harder to stay focused on tasks that are difficult, so a child who's having trouble learning to read will probably be a lot less attentive to the printed page than other children. As a result, it's sometimes hard to tell whether the child is inattentive because she can't read, or can't read because she's inattentive.

Environmental toxicity. Lead exposure, in particular, can create symptoms that resemble ADHD, especially in areas of academic performance. Any child who's suspected of having ADHD should have a blood test to rule out exposure to lead or other environmental contaminants.

Anxiety. Anxiety can closely mimic ADHD. When you're anxious or upset about something, it's hard to stay focused on the task at hand. And the nervous behaviors that often accompany anxiety—hair pulling, finger drumming, foot tapping, etc.—often look a lot like the hyperactivity of ADHD.

Just because your child is anxious doesn't mean he or she suffers from an anxiety disorder. It may be *situational*—that is, a normal, passing response to some specific situation or event such as starting school, moving to a new house, the birth of a sibling, family conflicts, or the death of a grandparent. You can usually distinguish this type of situational anxiety from ADHD because the symptoms tend to appear all at once. The symptoms of ADHD, by contrast, tend to be present from a very young age and remain consistent across a variety of settings: home, school, camp, vacation, church or synagogue, and so on.

In most cases, situational anxiety will pass all on its own as the child adjusts to the new situation; medication is only rarely necessary. Anxiety *disorders*, by contrast, involve long-standing anxiety, often without any apparent cause. Anxiety disorders often need to be treated with medication and counseling.

Sensorimotor integration. Researchers have only begun to explore this condition, and it's still poorly understood—especially by physicians. (Occupational therapists generally have more experience with it.) Sensorimotor integration (SMI) problems usually involve fine motor skills (such as writing and coloring) and gross motor skills (for example, throwing and catching a ball). SMI also involves *motor planning* issues—the ability to sequence motor activities appropriately. (Think, for example, of tying a shoelace: it requires a number of complex steps, which must be completed in a particular order.) In the classroom, SMI deficits will make it difficult for a child to complete written assignments promptly and accurately, and these difficulties, in turn, can make a child avoid or lose interest in such tasks. The end result often resembles the attentional problems we see with ADHD. Similarly, SMI makes it difficult to acquire athletic skills, diminishing the child's interest in sports and possibly causing social problems as well.

Seizure disorders. Seizures aren't always the obvious grand mal type that occur in epilepsy. "Subclinical" seizures can be so subtle as to be virtually unnoticeable, sometimes lasting only a few seconds and occurring without loss of consciousness. In some cases, they can look a lot like momentary inattention.

If there's a suspicion that attentional problems might be caused by a seizure disorder, an electroencephalogram (EEG) can confirm the condition, and it can usually be controlled well with antiseizure medication.

Mood disorders, including depression and bipolar disorders, can mimic ADHD as well. As with seizure disorders, one tip-off is that the problems come and go. But where seizures tend to occur randomly, mood-disorder symptoms are often cyclical. This ebb and flow typically isn't related to specific situations or circumstances; it's more like the tides or changing of the seasons. Also, depression often causes a characteristic change in sleep patterns.

Obsessive-compulsive disorder (OCD) is another mimicker of ADHD. But where most people with ADHD tend to be disorganized, one hallmark of OCD is a rigid, excessively organized style. So, for example, while a person with ADHD may have trouble finishing a test because she gets distracted, a child with OCD won't finish because she has to double-check and triple-check every answer. Also, people with OCD typically engage in many rituals: The foods on their plate can't be touching, for example, or they can't do their homework unless they have three no. 2 pencils on the table.

Someone who's lived with ADHD for a long time can end up acting very much like someone with OCD, because their ADHD often makes them feel out of control, and they may compensate by imposing excessive control over themselves and their environments.

Though outwardly similar, these two behaviors stem from very different causes. Here's one way to look at it: Someone with OCD may put her keys in exactly the same place every night because she's uncomfortable with the idea of their being anywhere else. Someone who's compensating for ADHD will put her keys in the same place every night because that's the only way she'll be able to find them in the morning.

Other medical conditions, such as hyperthyroidism, may also cause symptoms that resemble ADHD. So part of the assessment for ADHD must be a thorough physical examination to rule out such conditions.

What further complicates this whole picture is that these mimickers often *coexist* with actual ADHD. For example, a child may have ADHD, and his school problems are causing a secondary depression. That's why it's so important that the doctor who makes the diagnosis have extensive experience with ADHD in all of its various manifestations.

What can I do to help the doctor make an accurate diagnosis?

Patients and parents are well advised to become active partners with their physicians in arriving at a diagnosis. That doesn't mean you should shop around until you find a doctor who gives you the diagnosis you want to hear. But neither should you simply accept a diagnosis at face value. It's important to know how the doctor arrived at her conclusion—to know what other conditions she considered, and how she ruled them out; to understand what information she relied on to arrive at the diagnosis, and how she interpreted it.

Because the diagnosis of ADHD relies on the patient's history, you can collect information that will help the doctor arrive at the diagnosis. Ask the teacher and school counselor to provide written summaries of their own observations. Specifics are better than generalizations. It's better for the doctor to know that Joey sings songs during quiet time than simply to hear that he's disruptive.

Collect any documents—such as preschool evaluations—that may shed light on your child's past experiences. This patient history is essential to making the diagnosis of ADHD, because the doctor won't be able to tell much from observing your child in the office. A detailed history can also alert you and the doctor to other problems, including those that mimic ADHD and those that coexist with it.

And the best information you can offer is your own observations—the more specific, the better. If possible, keep a log or journal noting your child's behavior. This type of information is more useful than, say, a blanket statement that "he can't sit still."

If my child is being evaluated for ADHD, what questions should I ask?

The most important question is how the doctor approaches diagnosis and treatment of ADHD. There's a vast range of expertise in dealing with ADHD, especially among pediatricians and family practitioners.

As we've seen, treatment of ADHD involves a lot more than a prescription for Ritalin and a follow-up appointment six months later, and the proper treatment plan must begin with an accurate diagnosis. So if I were bringing my child to the doctor because I thought he might have ADHD, here are some of the questions I'd ask:

How will you find out whether my child has ADHD? The cornerstone of the ADHD diagnosis is a detailed history. The fact that a teacher is suddenly reporting behavioral problems, for example, isn't enough data to base the diagnosis on (in fact, chances are good that a sudden change in behavior *isn't* caused by ADHD). The doctor should look at the complete picture, now and in the past.

The doctor will probably perform a clinical examination, but this should be done to rule out other disorders, not to rule in ADHD. Because an office examination is one on one and a relatively infrequent experience, the symptoms of ADHD may not emerge during the visit.

Where do I find out about new research on ADHD? This question helps you gauge the doctor's interest in the topic. There is a lot of information available—seminars and conferences, continuing education programs and materials, and journal articles. Make sure your doctor is keeping up to date.

What treatment options are available? Often when one treatment—such as Ritalin—doesn't work, another will be effective. Make sure your doctor knows all of the alternatives, both medical and nonmedical.

What other conditions might be contributing to my child's difficulties? And how do you rule them out? This question will tell you whether the doctor is up to date on the latest findings regarding mimickers.

Where can I go for support? I've provided a list of resources at the end of the book; but this question is aimed at finding out how familiar the *doctor* is with them. If he or she isn't familiar with the resources available in the community—and conversely, if the support groups don't seem to know much about the doctor—you have to ask yourself whether this doctor is informed enough to assist you in getting the help you need.

When my child was diagnosed with ADHD, I took him for a second opinion. The second doctor looked at all the same records and concluded my child doesn't *have ADHD! Which one is right?*

Ultimately, the criteria for diagnosing ADHD are based on clinical judgments, which are somewhat subjective. In fact, much of medicine is based on good, trained clinical judgment, no matter what the specialty. For example, even an EKG must be interpreted, and different doctors may come to different conclusions.

So professionals may differ on how they make these judgments. Frankly, this subjectivity is one of the biggest problems of ADHD. Some critics even argue that since professionals can't agree on whether a given child has ADHD, the disorder itself can't be "real."

The difficulty lies not with the disorder but with the limitations of the tools we have to evaluate it. We don't yet have good objective tools to measure ADHD. So we must do the best we can with our eyes, our ears, and our clinical judgment.

I saw a television show that said there's no such thing as ADHD—that these kids are perfectly normal and it's all just a scheme to sell drugs and keep psychiatrists in business. How do I know this is a real disorder?

Attacks on psychiatry and medicine in general are nothing new, of course. At one time or another, most of the advances of modern medicine—from anesthesia to chemotherapy—have been characterized as ineffective, dangerous, even immoral.

There are hundreds of studies, going back forty years and more, on ADHD and the effects of medication. These studies show clear differences between people with ADHD and those without it. And they *consistently* show that there are dramatic improvements with medication. More recently, these clinical findings have been augmented by direct evidence of *physical differences* in the brain structure of people with symptoms of ADHD. And family studies show it to be a disorder that has a strong genetic component (see page 93).

Beyond the scientific evidence, however, is the evidence I see in my practice every day. For the typical child with ADHD, there's not much doubt that something is wrong. The parents have seen it. The teachers have seen it. Medical records, report cards, and school evaluations all show a consistent pattern of problems.

When I see adult patients with ADHD, they don't doubt the reality of the disorder. They offer dramatic accounts of its impact on their lives. Even before we confirm the diagnosis, they know there's something that has always made them different from other people—something that has caused problems for them throughout their lives.

Given the fact that these evaluations are subjective, how do you make the diagnosis?

First, I ask whether there's some other explanation for the patient's difficulties. For example, is the child's inattention in class related to something happening at home—a divorce, a death in the family, a new sibling? (One clue is whether there's been a marked *change* in behavior recently. The symptoms of ADHD are pervasive, and they're present over time.)

After ruling out other disorders, I'm left with the task of determining whether the symptoms add up to ADHD. And that's where we get into questions of how to interpret the data.

In many cases, the clinical history doesn't really leave much doubt about the diagnosis. If you had one hundred physicians who are experienced in ADHD evaluate the child, probably ninety of them would arrive at the same conclusion. The symptoms are such that they would meet any reasonable criteria for the disorder. Likewise, there are many children who clearly *don't* have ADHD—though they may have other difficulties.

Are relatives of a person with ADHD more likely to have the disorder?

Absolutely. For example, if you have ADHD, chances are fifty-fifty that your child will too. For that reason, when I'm making a diagnosis I always ask about other family members. It helps confirm the diagnosis for the patient, and it often alerts families to other potential cases of undiagnosed ADHD among siblings, parents, aunts, uncles, cousins, and grandparents.

So if other people in your family have problems related to attention (and remember, it can show up as anything from poor school and work performance to social problems to anxiety or depression), have them evaluated as well.

Are there any tests that are specifically designed for ADHD?

Yes. There are a number of assessment tools that run on a personal computer. But once again, these tests don't *prove* whether someone has ADHD. They simply provide another piece of the puzzle, which must be combined with all the others.

One of the most common types is the "continuous performance test." The test takes about ten minutes and it can be done right in the doctor's office. There are many variations, but the basic principles are the same for all of them: The patient sits at a computer as letters appear on the screen. When certain letters or sequences appear, the patient must respond by hitting a key on the keyboard.

My doctor says the best way to find out if my son has ADHD is to put him on Ritalin and see what happens—if he improves, he's got ADHD. If he doesn't, the problem is something else. Is he right?

Imagine that you went to a doctor because you thought you had high blood pressure. "Here," he says, "take these pills. If your blood pressure drops, that means it was high." Of course it doesn't—medication will make your blood pressure drop even if it was normal to begin with.

I don't know of any cardiologist who would prescribe treatment as a way of diagnosing hypertension. And yet some doctors "treat to diagnose" for ADHD. It's a bad idea for a number of reasons.

First, it exposes the patient to a medication he may not need. Second, it may obscure the real problem and delay appropriate treatment. Third, if it doesn't work, it creates a failure and erodes the child's trust in the judgment of parents and physicians.

It's important to remember that *just because the medication has an effect doesn't mean the patient has ADHD.* (Think again of the hypertension example.) In fact, Ritalin and other treatments for ADHD will improve the attentiveness even of normal children, so a medication-related behavior change doesn't confirm the diagnosis.

Interestingly, we find that people who don't have ADHD generally don't tolerate stimulants well over time. They quickly develop side effects and feel "drugged"—because they are. People with ADHD, by contrast, usually report a different experience: they tell us that the medication makes them feel normal.

As we've seen, inattentiveness can be caused by a lot of things other than ADHD. If it isn't ADHD, stimulants may improve attention but won't help the underlying disorder.

For example, a child who's depressed may be inattentive in class. Stimulants might improve her ability to focus, but she'll still be depressed.

Consider what happens when a child who doesn't have ADHD is "diagnosed" in this way. If his attention improves (and chances are it will regardless), he'll probably stay on the medication for years and years—perhaps his entire life. Later on, this condition will probably cause other problems—which will likely be ascribed to his "ADHD." Perhaps he'll get higher doses, or another medication. Eventually he may be classified as "treatment resistant"—one of those unfortunate people whose ADHD doesn't respond to treatment. Chances are, the child will grow up with a pretty dim view of medical science and its ability to help him. Even worse, he'll probably have a poor view of himself as well. And in all this time, his *real* disorder has gone untreated!

That's why it's vital to make a good diagnosis *before* treatment begins. In the end, the diagnosis will be a judgment call based on tests, observations, and the clinical history. If you medicate first and ask questions later, I think it's going to be very hard to find out what's going on.

While many people who actually have ADHD *aren't* getting treatment, there are many people being treated for ADHD who *don't* actually have it. Careful diagnosis can go a long way toward solving both of these epidemics.

Even though my doctor has explained the diagnosis to me, I'm still having trouble accepting that my child has ADHD. I think she just needs to try a little harder.

Unless you have ADHD yourself, it's hard to imagine just how hard your child *is* trying. Telling a child to "buckle down," "get organized," and "pay attention" isn't going to solve the problem. Nor will threats of punishment.

Over time, people with ADHD who aren't treated find ways of compensating for the disorder. I know someone who always left his gasoline cap sitting on top of the self-serve pump. After spending forty or fifty dollars on new gas caps, he finally tied one to the back of his car with a piece of string. He'd compensated for an attentional problem, but he hadn't overcome it.

But other "compensations" are more serious. For example, one way to compensate for classroom difficulties is to drop out of school. Another is to disrupt the class. One way to compensate for social difficulties is to take up solitary hobbies. Another way is to use drugs. Studies of adults with untreated ADHD show a high level of substance abuse—so *not* diagnosing and treating ADHD is a risky proposition.

Understandably, many parents would prefer to believe that their child's problems are neither serious nor permanent. They'd like to believe that she's having trouble in school because of a personality conflict with the teacher; that he climbed out his bedroom window because he's high-spirited.

Don't let those feelings prevent you from getting your child the help she needs.

When my pediatrician suggested that my child might have ADHD, I found I was angry—angry at my child, and angry at the doctor. Why would I feel this way?

It's hard for any of us to accept that there may be something wrong with our child—especially with a problem like ADHD, where there are no obvious physical signs of the disorder. Often the initial reaction is disbelief or anger. Often parents react by "shooting the messenger"—that is, directing their anger at the teacher or physician who brings them the news.

For parents, a diagnosis of ADHD represents a *loss*. Call it the "loss of the perfect child." Of course, we know that every child has her share of troubles. But on some deeper, unspoken, irrational level, we imagine our child to be perfect. And on an unconscious level, we lose that image of the perfect child when we accept the diagnosis of ADHD. And so we resist it.

For the parent of a child with ADHD, it's easy to underestimate this sense of loss. After all, we may tell ourselves, ADHD isn't a fatal illness. What's the big deal?

Well, it *is* a big deal. And parents need the opportunity to sort out their feelings about it. It's a perfectly normal reaction to deny the suggestion that your child has ADHD; to become angry at those who raise the issue; to try to "bargain" away the threat ("If you just work harder, you'll do fine"); and so on. We're simply working our way toward acceptance.

When I encounter such reactions among parents, I realize they're just part of the process. Often parents need some time before they can come to terms with the diagnosis. For example, a father may tell me that his child couldn't possibly have ADHD—that the problem is simply that the mother isn't strict enough. Six months later, however, after watching his child's behavior, he's ready to conclude that treatment just might be beneficial.

So if you find you don't believe the doctor, that you're angry at the teacher, that you're making deals with your child, understand that this is your mind's way of working things out. Give yourself time. And remember, ADHD is very treatable. With appropriate treatment, these kids usually do *great*.

CHAPTER 3

Identifying Treatment Options

After confirming the diagnosis, you and your doctor will begin to explore treatment options. Though the basic principles are straightforward, in practice treatment decisions are complicated by the presence or absence of other medical and developmental problems such as dyslexia, depression, or anxiety, as well as by the particular educational and family circumstances.

How is ADHD treated?

The cornerstone of a treatment plan for ADHD is medication—most often with the stimulant Dexedrine or Ritalin (see Chapter 4). But medication should be where treatment *begins*, not where it *ends*. It doesn't cure the disorder; rather, it controls the symptoms of ADHD. You also have to make changes in your child's surroundings to make the most of the opportunities that medication creates.

Let me give you an analogy. Imagine a child with bad eyesight went undiagnosed for years. He couldn't see the letters on the blackboard, so he never learned to read. He couldn't see the arithmetic problems in the workbook, so he never turned in his homework. He couldn't hit a softball because he couldn't see it coming.

Suppose further that as a result his teachers, his parents, and eventually the child himself concluded that he was mildly retarded and socially delayed.

Now imagine that this child finally gets a vision test and a new pair of glasses. His vision may be vastly improved, but he's still got a lot of catching up to do. He still has to learn how to read, how to do long division, how to hit a ball.

And he still has to address a lot of other issues as well: the lingering impression that he's "retarded." ("After all, we fixed his vision problems and he still can't keep up in class.") The disdain other kids have for his never-developed skills at sports. And underlying everything, his own feelings, developed over many years, that he's bad, lazy, or just stupid. In this hypothetical example, it's clear that a new pair of glasses doesn't solve these problems. The child will require remedial work to make up for lost ground. He will need help to "unlearn" the poor social skills that developed in response to his social isolation. And most important of all, he'll have to deal with his own feelings of self-esteem, which has been battered by years of frustration and failure.

So it is with ADHD medication. It's a *necessary* part of treatment, but it isn't *sufficient*. It creates the conditions for success, but it won't magically solve all of the problems surrounding ADHD.

Will treatment cure the condition?

No. There's no known cure for ADHD. It's a chronic condition, like asthma or diabetes, that must be managed throughout life.

If ADHD can't be cured, what are the goals of treatment?

To control the symptoms of ADHD and to permit the patient to achieve her full potential—from an educational, professional, personal, and emotional standpoint. A full life is an achievable goal; accepting anything less means that we have accepted limitations that don't need to be there.

These goals become the criteria by which we make treatment decisions and evaluate progress.

A treatment plan should embrace specific objectives, a means of measuring them and a timetable for achieving them. Here are some typical objectives:

Improve attention
Reduce impulsivity (if that's part of diagnosis)
Reduce/redirect hyperactivity (if present)
Enhance social skills and promote healthy peer interaction
Normalize academic performance
Maintain/promote self-esteem

To measure progress toward these objectives, you and your doctor may wish to set specific targets—for example, to bring reading up to grade levels, to complete twenty math problems within the assigned time, etc. Some objectives will be harder to measure, but even here they can help provide a direction. For example, you may wish to set as a social objective that your child will make one new friendship this month.

Besides medication, what other treatments are used for ADHD?

There are two other general approaches to treatment of ADHD, both of which involve counseling and training of children and parents. Both are based on the assumption that the ADHD child is lacking in certain skills and techniques.

The first, the "social learning" approach, is based on the behavior modification techniques pioneered by B. F. Skinner and other behavioral psychologists. Behavioral psychology focuses on outward, measurable behaviors and ways to influence them—for example, by rewarding the child for positive behaviors and punishing or ignoring negative behaviors. The "rewards" generally aren't money or toys, but rather praise and approval.

Another approach, "cognitive learning," aims to teach the child specific skills and techniques for problem solving and self-control. Unfortunately, however, it hasn't proved to be very effective for ADHD. (We'll take a closer look at both of these methods in Chapter 5.)

Where should I go for treatment?

Start with your child's regular physician. She will be the one who's most familiar with your child's development, and the one who's in the best position to prescribe and monitor treatment.

Who should prescribe and monitor treatment?

The integrated approach to treatment that I've described also requires the participation and support of many people—teachers, guidance counselors, psychologists and others. However, in most cases your pediatrician should be the one who coordinates and supervises the treatment. ADHD is a medical condition requiring medical treatment. Only your doctor can prescribe and monitor the medications that are the cornerstone of any treatment plan.

While that may seem self-evident, in the real world it can be hard to achieve. Because so many ADHD issues and behaviors involve the classroom, schools and teachers sometimes become the day-to-day coordinators and evaluators of treatment. While that's an appropriate role, make sure that your doctor doesn't abdicate his or her primary role in treatment. A good doctor will give great weight to the views of the school and other caregivers, but will arrive at diagnosis and treatment decisions independently after looking at *all* the data.

Do I need to see a specialist?

It depends. The primary care pediatrician or family prac-
titioner may be fine for many cases of ADHD, especially
where the diagnosis is clear, where there are no "comorbid"
disorders (that is, disorders that accompany and complicate
ADHD), and where the child responds well to medication
and has a supportive home and school environment.

However, because ADHD is often—in fact, usually—more
complex than it first appears, it's often a good idea to have a
specialist's involvement. One arrangement that often works
well is to use a specialist to make the diagnosis, look for
comorbid disorders, set up the medication plan, and, if necessary, modify it, and work with you and the school to ensure
that other supports are in place—an initial process that may
take, say, three to six months. Once these steps are completed
and as long as treatment is on track, the family doctor can
monitor treatment on an ongoing basis, with visits to the specialist once or twice a year to evaluate the progress.

What kind of specialist should I look for?

There are a variety of medical specialties and subspecialties
that work with ADHD, including child psychiatrists and developmental pediatricians. The most important criterion is how
many ADHD patients the specialist sees. Because it's such a
complex—and often subtle—disorder, there's no substitute
for lots of experience.

How do I know if I need to see a specialist?

Generally, you'll know if your child isn't getting better. Assuming your pediatrician has done the necessary evaluations to
arrive at an accurate diagnosis, and that a suitable treatment
plan is in place, you should see some changes pretty quickly.
(With Ritalin and Dexedrine, you can usually see an improvement in days. With other medications, it may take six weeks or

longer.) If you're not seeing any improvements, or if your child is having trouble with side effects or dosage schedules, you may have more complex treatment issues that a specialist should address.

In my experience, most pediatricians won't hesitate to call in a specialist for difficult cases. But your health plan may not be so quick to go along. It may discourage or even disallow your doctor from giving you a referral. If the plan won't authorize the referral, talk to your regular doctor; he may be able to get the health plan to reconsider if he explains why the referral is necessary. If that doesn't carry the day, and you and your doctor still believe the specialist's opinion is important, you may want to consider paying for it out of pocket. If cost is an issue, explain the situation when you make the appointment with the specialist; he may have some provision for a sliding scale based on the ability to pay.

Should my child be in psychotherapy?

Since ADHD is a physical disorder, psychological treatment— counseling, psychotherapy, group therapy, and the like—will be ineffective for ADHD.

Psychological therapies address only the psychological *consequences* of ADHD, not the medical condition itself. Many children with ADHD have low self-esteem because they don't do well in school, because they have difficulty in social situations, and so on. Families of children with ADHD often have lots of problems to deal with, and these kinds of issues may need to be addressed through counseling and psychotherapy. But it's important to understand that these psychological issues don't *cause* ADHD; rather, they are a *result* of it. So psychological counseling alone won't fix the underlying problem.

CHAPTER 4

Ritalin and Other Medications

If you mention ADHD medication, most people—doctors and consumers alike—think of Ritalin. In the United States, it's the overwhelming choice for treatment.

But it's not necessarily the best choice.

There are two key reasons for Ritalin's popularity. The first is tradition. Since its introduction in the 1960s, most early studies on the effects of stimulants on ADHD used Ritalin, in large part because it is short acting. Because it clears the system so quickly, it's an ideal drug to use in scientific studies: We can quickly see whether it works, and there are no lingering effects to throw off the study results.

Though these qualities make it easier to design and conduct a clean research study, they're often a disadvantage in the real world. In daily life, we *want* a medication to have lingering effects, so that it's easier to use and provides a consistent benefit rather than peaks and valleys.

But as treatment of ADHD became more widespread, it was only natural that doctors would prescribe the medications that had been studied the most extensively. There were mountains of scientific evidence showing that Ritalin was safe and effective. Though other stimulants such as Dexedrine (which was introduced in the 1930s) seemed to offer certain benefits over Ritalin, they were overshadowed by Ritalin's popularity and ease of use. So cautious physicians tended to prescribe the better-known treatment.

And as time went on, the process snowballed. The more doctors prescribed Ritalin for ADHD, the more experience they gained with it—making them even more likely to use it on new patients. And as more doctors started diagnosing and treating ADHD, it was only natural for them to look to Ritalin as well.

But as Ritalin became more widely used, its limitations have become more apparent, too. And that's now prompting a closer look at Dexedrine and other stimulants.

The second reason that Ritalin emerged as the more popular choice than Dexedrine is perception. Though both medications are stimulants and both are controlled substances, the public views Dexedrine as a far more dangerous drug. It's closely linked with drug abuse. And under its street name, speed, it's often implicated in illegal activities. (One reason: It's relatively easy to manufacture in small illegal labs.)

But in fact, Dexedrine and Ritalin are two of the safest medications administered to children—and both have the track record to prove it. In the very low doses used to treat ADHD, they don't create a risk of addiction or make children more predisposed to drug abuse problems later in life. (As a group, ADHD children are at greater risk of developing substance abuse problems, but this is because of the disorder, not the treatment. In fact, treatment actually *reduces* the likelihood that a child with ADHD will develop drug problems later on.)

None of this is to say that Ritalin isn't effective. It is. Ritalin may be the best choice for many people—but not for everyone. Most important, it isn't the *only* choice. That's good news for people for whom Ritalin doesn't work, and those who have trouble tolerating its side effects.

Dosage is another area in which tradition sometimes gets

in the way of effective treatment. Following the "standard" dosage regimens for ADHD medications is kind of like forcing everyone to wear a size $8^{1}/_{2}$ shoe. Just because it's right for most people doesn't mean it's right for everybody.

By tailoring the dosage and timing, it's often possible to improve vastly the effectiveness of these medications. Some people need larger than usual doses, but many actually get better control with *lower* doses. And by adjusting *when* these doses are given, one can get the maximum benefit of these medications—often with lower doses and fewer side effects.

Armed with these expanded options—more medications and more ways to administer them—you and your doctor can create an *individualized* medication regimen that will offer better and safer control.

The key to an effective medication plan for ADHD is to tailor the medication, dosage, and schedule to meet individual needs.

What medications are used to treat ADHD?

There are three general types of medication used to treat ADHD:

1. *Stimulants.* Stimulants are by far the most common treatment for ADHD—and usually the most effective.

Ritalin, Dexedrine and Adderall are the widely used and safe stimulants for treating ADHD. Another stimulant, Cylert (pemoline), should *not* be used to treat ADHD. It had been used to treat some cases that didn't respond to other medications. But it carries a risk of liver damage, and with other effective medications available, these risks outweigh the drug's potential benefits. As a result, the manufacturer and the Food and Drug Administration recommend that Cylert not be used in cases of ADHD.

2. *Antidepressants.* Parents often voice concerns about this second category of ADHD treatments. "Why would you give my child antidepressants if she's not depressed?" The answer lies

in the brain's chemistry. These drugs affect the brain chemistry in ways that can help control the symptoms of ADHD.

There are several categories, or classes, of antidepressants.

The first are known as *tricyclics*. Older tricyclics, such as Tofranil and desipramine, are effective, but they have many side effects (see chart).

A newer drug in this class, Wellbutrin, is emerging as a key treatment for ADHD when stimulants can't be used or don't work, as well as for cases of ADHD complicated by depression. It doesn't have the side effects of the older drugs and is therefore easier to tolerate. While experience with ADHD is still limited, it appears to have positive effects on attention as well as depression.

Another class of antidepressants known as *MAO inhibitors* has similar effects on these neurotransmitters, and they're now being tested as potential treatments for ADHD. However, dietary restrictions and associated risks make them an unlikely candidate for treating ADHD.

Yet another class, the *selective serotonin-reuptake inhibitors* (SSRIs) such as Prozac, Zoloft, and Paxil, are terrific for depression but *don't* work for ADHD. They are, however, used in combination with stimulants when ADHD and depression coexist—as they often do.

A new drug, Effexor (venlafaxine), is a *combined serotonin- and norepinephrine-reuptake inhibitor*. It does hold promise for treating ADHD, especially when it occurs with depression.

3. *Alpha-2-adrenoreceptor agonists.* This is another tongue twister, but you may recognize the medications themselves—Catapres (clonidine) and Tenex (guanfacine)—as widely used blood pressure medications. They're emerging as an alternative treatment for ADHD, especially atypical forms of ADHD that don't respond to stimulants. They're useful in cases where there's a lot of impulsivity.

Indeed, sometimes we use these drugs in combination with stimulants. Combination treatment can sometimes provide better control because the drugs work in different ways. In

COMPARING MEDICATION OPTIONS

Trade and Generic Name	Common Side Effects	Benefits	Drawbacks
Stimulants			
Ritalin (methylphenidate)	Insomnia Poor appetite Decreased appetite Headache Mood changes	Short-acting Works for most patients Good safety record Flexible Helps patients maintain focus	Frequent dosing is inconvenient Side effects may make it hard to stick with treatment May blunt emotions; may worsen anxiety
Ritalin-SR (methylphenidate)	Same as short-acting Ritalin	Eliminates midday dose Good safety record	Same as above Less effective than short-acting Ritalin and other stimulants
Dexedrine (dextroamphetamine)	Insomnia Decreased appetite Nausea Headache Mood Changes	Fast-acting Provides more "natural" response (patient "feels like herself")	Not tolerated by everybody; can produce angry or edgy reaction
Dexedrine spansules	Same as Dexedrine	Good long-acting forms: long duration of action eliminates midday dose	Same as Dexedrine

Medication	Side Effects	Benefits	Cautions
Adderall *(mixed salts of amphetamines)*	Same as Dexedrine	Provides more consistent control with long duration of action Often better tolerated than Dexedrine	Same as Dexedrine
Tricyclic Antidepressants			
Tofranil *(imipramine)*	Dry mouth Constipation Decreased appetite Nausea Dizziness Constipation Rapid heartbeat	Long-acting Effective for comorbid depression and anxiety	Takes up to several weeks to work Must be taken consistently; medication is continually circulating in the bloodstream Doesn't work immediately Not as effective as stimulants
Norpramin *(desipramine)*	Fewer side effects than Tofranil	Same as Tofranil	Same as Tofranil
New-Generation Tricyclic			
Wellbutrin SR *(bupropion)*	Insomnia Rash Nausea	Easy dosing Long acting More effective than other tricyclics for attentional problems	Not as effective "focus" as stimulants

Trade and Generic Name	Common Side Effects	Benefits	Drawbacks
Combined Serotonin- and Norepinephrine-Reuptake Inhibitor			
Effexor (venlafaxine)	Fewer than traditional tricyclics and stimulants	Fast response, long-acting Especially good for ADHD/depression	May not be as effective as stimulants Must be taken consistently
Alpha-2-Adrenoreceptor Agonists			
Catapres (clonidine)	Sleepiness (only with pill, not patch) Low blood pressure	Good control of behavior and impulses Helps control comorbid tic disorders. Promotes sleep	Short-acting Could cause rebound hypertension if discontinued suddenly
Tenex (guanfacine)	Low blood pressure	Same as Catapres; longer acting	Doesn't affect focus; only impulsivity No pills to take (for patch) Same as Catapres

addition, they can help promote sleep, so they can counter the tendency of the stimulants to interfere with falling asleep. They may, however, cause nightmares.

❏ Ritalin and Other Stimulants

What are the effects of stimulants on ADHD?

Numerous studies have shown that stimulants such as Ritalin and Dexedrine improve the symptoms of ADHD for the overwhelming majority of patients who take them. The improvements are seen regardless of whether the patient is preschool age, elementary school age, adolescent, or adult.

Stimulants improve attentiveness; reduce hyperactivity, restlessness, and distractibility; and improve the ability to follow directions and stay on task.

By controlling aggressiveness and impulsiveness, these medications also have a dramatic impact on social relationships, both within the family and among peers. One study found that ADHD boys who started taking Ritalin were more likely to be rated as "cooperative" and "fun to be with" than they had been previously. Ritalin also reduces the incidence of verbal and physical aggression. And researchers find that when children are treated, parents and siblings respond with more warmth, more contact, less criticism, and greater cooperativeness.

The results are similar in the classroom: About 75 percent of ADHD children who are treated with stimulants show marked improvement according to teachers' evaluations. And these findings are borne out by measurements of the children's physical level of activity. Some research studies have used electronic monitors to measure ADHD children's level of activity, and they find that activity drops significantly with medication, both during daytime hours and during sleep. In fact, these changes can be detected as early as thirty minutes after the very first dose.

What are the benefits of stimulants for ADHD?

Of all the drugs used to treat ADHD, stimulants are the most consistently effective. What's more, they work quickly—often you can see changes starting with the very first dose.

In addition, stimulants are short-acting. They don't build up in the system. That makes it easier to fine-tune doses to get the best control. And it's reassuring to know that they clear the body quickly.

Also, stimulants have a decades-long track record of safe use in the treatment of ADHD. In fact, we know from this experience that they're among the safest medications prescribed to children.

What are the drawbacks?

While most people do well on stimulants, a small minority of patients can't tolerate the side effects (see discussion of side effects below), even after dosages are adjusted.

Another drawback is that control tends to be uneven with short-acting stimulants, because they do clear the system so quickly. As we'll see, you can time dosages to prevent this roller-coaster effect, but it can be a lot of work to maintain this schedule.

How do stimulants work?

Each nerve cell has two ends—a head and a tail, if you will. At the head, the cell manufactures chemicals known as neurotransmitters. As their name implies, these chemicals *transmit* an impulse from one nerve to the next.

The nerve cell stores these neurotransmitters until a signal reaches it; then it releases them from the head of the cell. Some of the neurotransmitters attach themselves to *receptors* on the next nerve's tail. They fit into these receptors like a key into a lock, triggering a signal in the second nerve. This signal, in turn, travels to the head of the second cell, where the process happens again. This chain reaction of chemical and electrical signals transmits the impulse along the nerve pathway.

To fire the second nerve, the first nerve has to release enough neurotransmitters to bind with the receptor sites. Normally, it releases more than necessary. After the neurotransmitters have done their job, the original cell recaptures some of them, storing them to be used again. But some of the neurotransmitters are destroyed. Thus, if you fire the nerves repeatedly, the cells deplete their supply of neurotransmitters and the nerves can't transmit signals as effectively until they manufacture more.

We're not quite sure what happens in ADHD, but it appears to involve a deficit in the neurotransmitters. The most powerful evidence for this idea is the fact that stimulants—and Dexedrine in particular—are close chemical cousins of the neurotransmitters and fit into the receptor "locks" quite nicely. It may be that they make up for a chronic deficit in natural neurotransmitters. Or the problem might be on the receiving end, with receptors that aren't sensitive enough. Or the medications might prompt nerve cells to produce or release more neurotransmitters. We simply don't know, because we don't yet have tools that can look at these processes on a chemical level in the brain.

What this complex process really boils down to is this: ADHD throws this electrical-chemical messenger system out of whack, creating "static" in the transmission. It's sort of like getting a weak signal from your television antenna—the picture gets through, but it's fuzzy. The medication acts to make the signal stronger so that the static disappears.

Chances are, the reason we see so many mimickers—and so many conditions that occur along with ADHD—is that so many factors can disrupt this delicate neurotransmitter balance and put static on the system. Depression, for example, upsets the balance of neurotransmitters, as do anxiety and other mood disorders. On the other hand, learning disorders such as dyslexia are not caused by alterations in this communication system, and therefore do *not* respond to medication.

What are the side effects of stimulants?

The most common side effects are insomnia, decreased appetite, weight loss (probably as a result of appetite suppression), headache, increased heart rate, slight increases in blood pressure, and an increased tendency to cry. Less common side effects include heart palpitations, dizziness, and anxiety.

With the doses used for treatment of ADHD, these side effects tend to be mild if they occur at all. If they do occur, they often disappear after a few weeks as the body adjusts. And if they persist, they can usually be managed by reducing the dosage temporarily or changing the time at which the child takes the medication (e.g., giving the medication earlier in the day to prevent insomnia). If insomnia still occurs from time to time, Benadryl at bedtime can help promote sleep. (Though Benadryl is usually used for allergies, it has a sedative effect and is safe for children.) Upset stomach can usually be managed by giving the medication with milk or about an hour after meals.

There have been several case reports of mania or psychotic episodes; it appears that in at least some incidents the drug worsened an underlying psychotic condition. Although high doses of stimulants can trigger seizures in people with epilepsy, the doses used for ADHD are usually too low to have any such effect. In fact, children who have both epilepsy and ADHD are usually treated with stimulants and an anticonvulsant medication.

Why prescribe a stimulant for a child who's already hyperactive? Shouldn't you give him something to calm him down instead?

The short answer is that we don't use these medications in the way most people think of stimulants. We don't prescribe them as "pep pills" or to overcome fatigue. In fact, the doses are so low that you're unlikely to see any "stimulant" effect at all.

In a sense, the confusion comes from the term *hyperactivity*. The problem with ADHD children isn't that they have too much energy; it's that their energy tends to be uncontrolled. In fact, all of the key symptoms of ADHD—the attentional problems, the impulsivity, and the hyperactivity—reflect difficulties in controlling mental and physical activity.

If you look at studies of brain chemistry, you can see this loss of control reflected on the most basic cellular level. In people with ADHD, the cells in the part of the brain that control these behaviors have trouble communicating with one another. Treatment stimulates this "controlling" or "filtering" portion of the brain, making it work more normally.

What are the odds that treatment with stimulants will be effective?

These drugs are effective in more than 90 percent of cases, but about 15 percent of patients experience side effects that preclude their use. Sometimes these side effects can be overcome by switching medications or adjusting dosages. The bottom line is that treatment is successful in about 90 percent of cases.

How long have these drugs been in use?

The use of stimulants to treat ADHD and related disorders can be traced back as far as 1937. When a physician studying children in a residential treatment program gave them Dexedrine, he found that the children—contrary to expectations—showed lower activity levels, better behavior, and improved school performance. In the 1960s, more rigorous studies, again looking at students in a residential school, found that the use of these drugs resulted in fewer conduct problems and better behavior and school performance.

However, at the time the concept of ADHD as a distinct disorder had not yet evolved; at this point it was simply known that for some children with conduct and school performance problems, stimulants seemed to help.

Ritalin was first commercialized in the early 1960s as a memory aid for geriatric patients, and some years later researchers, noting its chemical similarity to the amphetamines used in the earlier studies, began exploring its use for children with behavior and academic difficulties.

What are the pros and cons of methylphenidate (Ritalin) versus Dexedrine or Adderall?

Though Ritalin is still the most widely prescribed treatment for ADHD in the United States, more and more physicians are coming to view Dexedrine and Adderall as the treatments of choice for ADHD.

As we've seen, Ritalin has been well studied, and its effectiveness well established. In addition, it takes effect quickly and clears the system quickly, which may make it easier to adapt the dosing schedule to your child's needs. (For example, if your child has a "slump" in the evening, a late-afternoon dose of Ritalin will help, while still clearing the child's system by bedtime. With a longer-acting medication, you don't have this flexibility.)

However, Ritalin's short duration of action makes it more difficult to manage the typical child's school day. One dose lasts about three hours, so if the child takes the dose with breakfast, then gets dressed, waits for the bus, rides the bus to school, and sits through homeroom, he or she may be halfway through the first dose before the school day really gets started. That means the late-morning classes will be difficult. And if your child's school is one that will not administer a lunchtime dose, the afternoon is likely to be even worse.

In some children, Ritalin also has a tendency to blunt emotions. "He seems sad," a parent may tell me, but if you ask the child, he doesn't say he feels sad. It's more a feeling of distance, of being a little bit removed from things. "He doesn't seem like himself," another parent told me, and I think that's a better description.

This effect doesn't happen in every child who takes Ritalin; in fact, it doesn't happen in most of them. But if you see these effects in your child, there's a simple solution: Ask your doctor to switch to another medication. Dexedrine doesn't seem to have this side effect, and it's more convenient to administer because it's longer-acting.

Dexedrine's chief drawback, frankly, is its reputation. On the street, of course, Dexedrine is known as "speed," and when abused it is addictive and dangerous.

However, years of research have demonstrated that Dexedrine, as it's used in the treatment of ADHD, is safe and non-addictive. In people with ADHD, clinical doses of Dexedrine don't make you "high." They don't create drug dependence. And they don't create tolerance—that is, you don't need bigger and bigger doses to produce the same effects.

In fact, this is one of the ways we know that ADHD is a disorder of normal brain metabolism: Whereas normal people develop tolerance to stimulants, people with ADHD don't. It seems that while stimulants throw the brain chemistry out of balance in most people, they make it more normal in people with ADHD.

How well does the long-acting form of Ritalin work?

The long-acting form of Ritalin requires only one dose every six to eight hours. Its primary benefit is that the school doesn't have to administer a lunchtime dose. For that reason, we may use it if the child is in a school that refuses to give the lunchtime medication. But I find—as do many of my colleagues—that it doesn't offer the same degree of effectiveness as standard Ritalin.

My doctor suggested a new stimulant called Adderall. What is it?

Adderall is a new formulation of dextroamphetamine (like Dexedrine) and amphetamines. We're using it with many of our patients, because a single dose offers good, consistent control over a longer period of time—six to seven hours. It accomplishes this by combining four closely related types of stimulants, some of which work more quickly and some more slowly.

This formulation—combining slow- and fast-acting components—is different from the long-acting Ritalin, which uses a single drug but releases it gradually over time. We find that it works much better, and it's a good way to avoid both the midday dosage and the peaks and valleys that we see with short-acting stimulants.

My child's doctor says to take the pills before eating. But then my son isn't hungry. Why can't he take it after meals?

Food interferes with the ability of the body to absorb stimulants, so the medications often don't work as well if you take them after you've eaten. In addition, some foods interfere more than others, so you may see the drugs acting inconsistently, depending on the menu. For example, citrus juice interferes with Ritalin.

But the standard recommendation to take them before meals can cause problems for some patients. As you pointed out, they can suppress appetite. Also, if breakfast is early in your household, that can throw off the medication schedule for the entire day, because the medication may start wearing off in mid-morning.

There are some other options, though. For example, we often recommend taking the drug *after* meals. The only caution is not to take them too soon after; wait at least an hour.

Some people also feel nauseous if they take a stimulant on an empty stomach. In that case, you can take it with milk.

It's important to find the dosage strategy that has the least impact on appetite, because poor nutrition can make ADHD symptoms worse (not to mention the impact on growth). For example, researchers have found that children who get protein at breakfast (for example, from milk or yogurt) do better in school than those who don't. For children with ADHD, that difference can be critical.

How necessary is the evening dose of Ritalin (or other short-acting stimulants)?

There's no black-and-white answer. Again, the key is to work with your doctor to create a plan that works for you.

Some parents using short-acting stimulants find it beneficial to skip the last dose; it gives the child a chance to wind down and fall asleep more easily. Other parents find exactly the opposite effect: The loss of control turns every evening into a battle.

So the best guide is your own experience. However, I do think that *most* children—not all—do better when medication levels are relatively steady throughout the day. ADHD isn't a disorder that happens just during school hours, and the fluctuations can be very disorienting and demoralizing. You can think of medication kind of like the brakes on your car. It gives you control. Imagine driving a car where your brakes are unreliable—where they work for a little while, then don't, then start working again. In some ways, it's worse than having no brakes at all, because you never know what to expect.

In many cases, that's what happens with ADHD. The sense of control—the ability to know what to expect—is often a critical part of building self-esteem and confidence, and preventing anxiety. I am a strong advocate for consistent medication.

Do stimulants cause tics?

There have been concerns over the years that stimulants may promote tics—involuntary muscle twitches of the face and body—in some children with ADHD. But it's not that simple.

Tics can range from something as mild and virtually unnoticeable as a slight facial twitch (or even excessive blinking) to involuntary spasms of the entire head or limbs or both. In a related condition, Tourette's syndrome, tics may be accompanied by involuntary outbursts of obscene or offensive speech. That's the bad news. The good news is that the vast majority of tic disorders are well toward the milder side of this scale. Even in cases of Tourette's syndrome, severe symptoms such as verbal outbursts are quite uncommon. Further good news: Tics don't really cause any physical harm, though severe ones may cause social problems. And best of all, most tics can be controlled with medication.

In a small minority of cases, stimulants may trigger tics. It's not clear whether they actually *cause* the tic, or simply bring a preexisting condition out into the open. There's evidence that tic disorders may mimic ADHD in their early stages; in these cases, the tic might have developed whether we'd treated the patient with stimulants or not. Even though it looks as if the medication *caused* the tics, in such cases they would have emerged *regardless* of whether the child had been medicated or not.

Nonetheless, we do see a link between stimulants and tics, and it does create a dilemma.

It requires a careful weighing of risks and benefits. If the child has shown evidence of tics in the past, or if there's a family history (tic disorders tend to run in families), we proceed very carefully. In such cases, we usually begin with ADHD treatments other than stimulants.

Catapres (clonidine) or Tenex (guanfacine) are often the first choice. They're relatively safe, and in many cases it can control both tic disorders *and* ADHD. (Other drugs, such as haloperidol or respiridol, are more effective than clonidine for tics and Tourette's syndrome, but they have a lot of side effects. So they're usually used only in more severe cases, and only if Catapres doesn't work.)

If Catapres, Tenex or other similar medications don't control the ADHD symptoms, we do look at using stimulants. But we do so carefully, weighing the risks and consequences of exacerbating a tic against the risks and consequences of not treating the ADHD.

It's not a straightforward choice. For example, while stimulants may make tics worse, they sometimes make them *better.* Here's why: Tics are usually stress related. For example, many parents say their child's tics get worse on Sunday nights—but if there's no school the next day, the tic magically moves to Monday night instead. So if ADHD is creating a stressful situation for the child, treatment may calm the tic by reducing school-related anxiety. (One helpful hint: A good night's sleep provides an enormous benefit for both ADHD and tics—and it's a risk-free therapy.)

I don't want to leave you with the impression that you shouldn't be concerned about the relationship of tics and stimulants. Rather, I'm suggesting that it isn't a black-and-white issue, and it must be managed carefully. One approach that often works well is to treat the ADHD with stimulants and manage any tics with Catapres.

The issue can get complicated, but the alternative—not treating the ADHD at all—will have much more severe consequences. It's a matter of balancing risks and benefits.

Isn't it true that stimulants stunt growth?

Stimulants do affect the *rate* at which children grow, but numerous studies suggest that these children *end up* at the same height.

Studies of children treated two years or more with Ritalin or Dexedrine show a "decrease in weight velocity" on standard age-adjusted growth rate charts. In plain English, they don't gain weight as quickly. The effects are more pronounced with Dexedrine, presumably because it's longer-acting. Although researchers haven't identified exactly why this effect occurs, the most likely explanation is the drugs' effects on appetite.

Understandably, parents are more concerned about height

than weight. Fortunately, most of the research has found minimal, if any, long-term effects on height from ADHD therapy. One study of sixty-five children found that initially they grew more slowly, but caught up during adolescence. By age eighteen, these patients had reached their predicted heights, based on their parents' heights. Other studies have confirmed these findings, showing that stimulants had only a mild and temporary effect on weight and "only rarely interfered with height acquisition."* And they have *no* impact on growth after puberty.

However, keep in mind that these studies look at *group* statistics, not *individuals*. It's possible that the effects may be more pronounced in some children and less so in others. That's why it's important that your child's growth be monitored regularly by your pediatrician. Most monitor height and weight from infancy onward against standard charts. These charts measure percentiles—for example, a child who falls in the fiftieth percentile for height and weight will be taller and heavier than 50 percent of children his age. It's not so important how quickly your child grows—this changes all the time—but whether this percentile score remains relatively steady. A change of a few points isn't significant, but if your child's height or weight percentile begins to drop noticeably, it's a reason to look more closely at whether the medication is affecting growth. Studies show that a drop in the weight percentile usually happens before declines in the height percentile, so it can give you an early warning.

Also, research suggests that the effects on height and weight may be more pronounced on larger children. So if your child tends toward the upper end of the charts, he or

---

*L. L. Greenhill et al. "Medication treatment strategies in the MTA studies: relevance to clinicians and researchers." *Journal of the American Academy of Child and Adolescent Psychiatry* 1996; 35:1304–13. This article describes the role of psychostimulant medication in the treatment of attention deficit hyperactivity disorder. Included are the drugs' putative mechanisms of action, pharmacology, toxicology, indications for their use, short-term and long-term actions, adverse effects, specific dosing regimens, therapeutic monitoring techniques, alternative medications, and drug interactions.

she may be at greater risk. On the other hand, a differential of a few pounds in weight or a fraction of an inch in height will be less of a concern in a child who's well above the average norms to begin with.

Should we consider "medication holidays" to offset these effects?

Children tend to make up for slowed growth when treatment is discontinued temporarily (at least through adolescence). That's one reason why many pediatricians suggest a "drug holiday" during summer vacations. In the summertime or on weekends, the thinking goes, the child has fewer academic demands and can "burn off" excess energy with sports and other activities.

But I'm concerned that these "holidays" may actually do more harm than good. If you assume that ADHD is a disorder that affects only classroom learning, then medication holidays make sense. But we know that isn't so. ADHD affects every aspect of a child's life.

Take summer camp, for example. If your child's ADHD is making it difficult for him to make and keep friends, to participate in sports like softball and soccer, to learn how to swim, or to listen to his or her counselor, it's not much of a holiday. If your child's weekends are spent fighting with siblings and parents or bouncing off the walls, I'm not sure you're doing him or her any favors by withholding medication.

If you look at ADHD as a chronic physical disorder that must be managed with medication, you can begin to see the flaw in the logic of these holidays. Nobody suggests that children with diabetes should take a "holiday" from their insulin.

On the other hand, I understand the concerns that parents feel about keeping a child on medication. And there may be some benefit to forgoing medication over the summer to let growth "catch up" to normal—though there's no good evidence one way or the other.

As I've said before, one must balance the risks against the benefits, and the analysis will be different in every individual case. If you have a child with mild ADHD symptoms—perhaps without the hyperactive component—and these symptoms are usually an issue only when it comes to schoolwork, then a medication holiday may make a lot of sense. If you have a child with severe attentional difficulties, a lot of aggression, and significant social problems, the scales may tip toward more consistent medication.

There are no hard-and-fast rules, no right or wrong answers. The most important thing is always to keep in mind that the treatment of ADHD ultimately is about self-esteem and success, not about specific symptoms and medication regimens.

Why did my pharmacist refuse to refill my prescription?

Stimulants, including both Ritalin and Dexedrine, are "controlled substances" subject to legal restrictions. Because these drugs have a potential for abuse, the federal government imposes certain restrictions on how they're prescribed and dispensed. One prohibits automatic refills—not because there's anything wrong per se with taking these drugs over long periods of time, but to prevent people from getting refills just to sell or abuse, and to ensure that they're being used under the continuing supervision of a physician.

What effect does caffeine have on ADHD?

For most people, not much. Although caffeine is a mild stimulant, its effects simply aren't strong enough to affect ADHD.

Can stimulants be used if my child is also on other medications?

It depends on the medication.

Stimulants should never be used in combination with MAO in-

hibitor antidepressants. Combining these drugs can raise blood pressure to extremely dangerous, even fatal, levels.

Less severe drug interactions can occur with stimulants and asthma medications—specifically, medications such as theophylline that are taken by mouth. Because these medications are chemically related to stimulants, the combination can cause such side effects as palpitations, weakness, dizziness, and agitation. If your child has asthma, ask your doctor if it's possible to switch him or her to an inhalant medication to prevent these effects.

Stimulants such as Ritalin will also raise blood levels of certain other medications, such as anticonvulsants and antidepressants such as fluoxetine (Prozac), increasing their effects. If your child is taking these or other medications, ask your doctor or pharmacist about potential interactions and whether the dosages should be adjusted. Stimulants may interact with cold medications (e.g., Sudafed), making the effects of both stronger.

My daughter was doing great on stimulants for several months. But all of a sudden they just stopped working. Why?

There is a possibility that your child has a mimicking disorder. We find that when people have something that looks like ADHD but isn't, the medications sometimes work for a while and then peter out.

But from this description—in which the medications just stopped working all at once—I would suspect another factor: allergies. Allergy reactions release *histamines*, chemicals that interfere with the action of stimulants.

Although I've seen no studies on the interaction between allergies and ADHD, I can tell you that every spring, I get a number of phone calls from parents telling me that their child's medication is no longer working. After looking at possible factors—for example, a sudden growth spurt or a change in the classroom environment—we often find that the only thing that's changed is the weather. And when I ask the parents if the child's allergies are bad, they almost invariably say yes.

You and your doctor might consider this simple solution: You don't need to increase the stimulant dosage. Just use antihistamines to control the allergy. That usually restores the effectiveness of the ADHD medications during allergy season.

The teachers say my child is doing better, but I don't see any change at home. Why not?

The reason may be your child's medication schedule. For example, if your child is taking Ritalin in the morning and at noon, the effects have probably worn off by 3 or 4 P.M., about the time your child is coming home from school. This phenomenon is common enough in ADHD to have its own name—"behavioral rebound"—and sometimes the symptoms are even more pronounced than before treatment began. Ask your doctor to consider three-times-a-day dosing; a final dose after school will carry you through to bedtime.

❐ Antidepressants

What are the effects of antidepressants on ADHD?

Though antidepressants are chemically different from stimulants, they have similar effects on the key symptoms of ADHD: attentiveness, impulsivity, and hyperactivity.

Compared to the stimulants, antidepressants are slightly less effective, and they have higher risk of serious side effects. In addition, antidepressants must accumulate in the body to be effective; stimulants don't. For all these reasons, most doctors prefer to start with stimulant therapy and substitute antidepressants if the stimulants don't work or have unacceptable side effects. For people who have both ADHD and depression, antidepressants are the preferred choice.

What are the key benefits?

Antidepressants have some advantages over stimulants. They work for longer periods of time, so it's often possible to use twice-a-day dosings (morning and evening), eliminating the problem of giving doses during the school day. Also, the doctor can use a blood test to measure the amount of medication actually circulating in the bloodstream; this can be useful to determine whether the drug is working as it should and to monitor for too high levels.

What are the drawbacks?

The biggest drawback with these drugs is that they have to build up in your system to be effective. That makes it harder to fine-tune treatment. Also, you can't stop treatment suddenly; you have to taper off the medication level over three to four weeks.

And because they have to build up over time, they never completely clear out of your system. Stimulants, by contrast, are completely eliminated from your body within a few hours.

In general, tricyclic antidepressants are better suited for adolescents and adults than children. When children use them, the best strategy is to start with a low dose (for example, 10 to 25 mg of desipramine) broken up into three or more doses if possible, then increasing the dosage gradually over several weeks, up to a maximum of 125 mg a day. Most patients won't need such high doses, however, and by phasing in the dose this way, the doctor can monitor the medication for its effectiveness and potential side effects.

Though the risks of heart problems are slight, most experts recommend that anyone taking tricyclic antidepressants get an electrocardiogram (EKG) regularly. The EKG, which monitors the heart's rhythm, can provide early warnings of heart-related problems.

How do these drugs work?

Antidepressants, like stimulants, affect how your brain uses neurotransmitters. They seem to work by preventing the breakdown of neurotransmitters after they're released from the nerve ending. As a result, they increase the amount of neurotransmitters that are present between nerve cells, thereby helping to transmit the signals more effectively.

Though they work by a different mechanism than the stimulants, the end result is largely the same: more neurotransmitters are available to transmit messages between nerve cells.

What kinds of side effects can I expect to see?

Antidepressants' side effects are usually less severe than those of stimulants. The most common side effects—occurring in about one fourth to one third of cases—include dry mouth, decreased appetite, headaches, nausea, fatigue, dizziness, and insomnia. Occasionally they increase heart rate and blood pressure, but these effects are usually insignificant at the low doses used to treat ADHD.

Can these medications be used if my child is on other medications?

It depends on the medication and type of antidepressant. One strategy we sometimes use for ADHD is to combine certain antidepressants with stimulants. That allows us to use lower doses of each, and take advantage of their complementary benefits: Because antidepressants are long-acting, we can use lower doses of them to provide a baseline level of focus. But stimulants provide better focus, so we can use them as supplements—again in lower doses—at critical times such as school to provide more complete control. This approach often allows us to prevent the ups and downs that occur with short-acting stimulants, and can help reduce side effects since we're using lower doses of both medications.

☐ Alpha-2-Adrenoreceptor Agonists

What are the effects of Catapres and Tenex on ADHD?

These drugs are most widely used as blood pressure medications, but they're seeing use as an alternative to stimulants for treatment of ADHD. They work best in children with a lot of hyperactivity and aggression, and those who tend to be overfocused rather than simply distractible or inattentive. They're also drugs of choice when ADHD appears with tics or Tourette's syndrome (a disorder that may include both vocal and body tics). In fact, they're used to treat Tourette's syndrome even when it doesn't involve ADHD. They're often used in combination with stimulants.

Catapres is available as a skin patch. Placed on the torso, it provides a slow, sustained release of the drug. This helps avoid sleepiness and provides good behavioral control.

What are the key benefits?

As with the stimulants, they don't seem to create tolerance. Also, they don't appear to suppress appetite the way the stimulants do. Catapres may help a child fall asleep when given in the evening—a benefit for many children with ADHD. Tenex has no effect on sleep.

Although the research is still preliminary, these drugs may emerge as the treatment of choice for a particular subtype of ADHD: *overfocused* behavior.

What are the drawbacks?

These medications have little effect on the inattentiveness that's seen with classic ADHD. But since attentional problems and impulsivity can occur in the same child, combining them with stimulants may offer the best control. The two types of drugs can be taken together safely.

Another possible drawback: Unlike stimulants, which take effect immediately, your child may have to take these drugs for several weeks before their full effects become apparent. However, most begin to experience some improvement within days.

Also, these drugs can (rarely) make depression worse, so the doctor has to monitor mood carefully in children who have ADHD and depression.

What kinds of side effects can I expect to see?

Side effects are uncommon, and generally mild when they do occur. They include drowsiness, low blood pressure and resulting dizziness, headache, nausea, depression, and effects on heart rhythm. Most side effects can be managed by reducing the dosage.

The most common side effect is drowsiness. If your child has trouble getting up and staying awake, it probably means that the medication levels are being increased too quickly. Your doctor will likely reduce the dosage and then increase it again more gradually.

These drugs also tend to lower blood pressure. A mild drop in blood pressure usually produces no symptoms, but bigger drops may cause dizziness, especially when the child stands up quickly after sitting or lying down. This and other side effects—which may include headaches and nausea—usually go away after a few weeks of treatment. More serious, but rare, are reports that these drugs may worsen depression or trigger it in a child with a family history of mood disorders. Catapres has also caused irregular heartbeats in adults, but its heart effects in children and adolescents haven't been studied yet in any detail.

If your child has to be taken *off* Catapres or Tenex—for example, because it isn't helping or because of side effects—your physician has to do it gradually. Like most blood pressure medications, these can cause "rebound hypertension"—that is, a sudden and potentially dangerous rise in blood pressure—if it's discontinued too quickly.

What are the odds that treatment will be effective?

These drugs are effective in about 70 percent of cases of impulsivity. They are not particularly effective for focus and attention.

Can these medications be used if my child is on other medications?

Yes. They have few known contraindications or interactions with other drugs or with foods.

What are the typical dosages?

Traditionally, Clonidine tablets are given in the evening, because they act as a sedative. But the medication usually works best when it's administered in several small doses during the day rather than a single larger dose. To reduce the sedative effects, doses should be low at the beginning of treatment—for example, half of a 0.1 mg tablet a day for Catapres—and gradually increased to get the maximum benefit. Typically, dosages for a child will be about 0.15 to 0.3 mg—that is, three half or full tablets—a day. For adolescents the dosages will likely be a little higher. In most cases, the maximum dose won't be more than 0.5 mg a day.

Catapres is available in a skin patch as well as a pill, so it can be used in children who have trouble taking medication. The patch doesn't cause sleepiness either, so it's a useful alternative for those who can't tolerate the pills' sedative effects. Usually, however, the doctor will prescribe pills at the beginning, until tolerance to the sedative effects are established. A single patch usually lasts for four to five days. Some develop a mild skin irritation where the patch is attached; it's easily treated with a low-dose corticosteroid cream.

☐ General Medication Issues

Which medications work best?

There's no single answer to this question. In most patients, stimulants emerge as the drug of choice, but in others they don't work at all. Even within these categories, the responses of individual patients can be very different, often for no discernible reason. One child may do fine on Ritalin but not Dexedrine; for another it may be just the reverse. One may experience troubling side effects while his classmate has no such side effects.

How, then, do doctors know which medications to use?

Unfortunately, there's no good way to predict the response to a type of medication or a dosage schedule. So don't be surprised by some degree of trial and error as you try to get it right.

Each medication has its pros and cons, and we'll look at each of them in turn later in this chapter.

Are generics equivalent?

In my experience, no—especially the generic equivalent of Ritalin. If your health care prescription plan restricts you to certain medications, you may have trouble getting brand name Ritalin covered. Different plans have different rules, but if you encounter this problem, it's sometimes possible to win an exception if your doctor documents that the generic medication wasn't effective or files an appeal with the insurer.

How soon can I expect to see results?

With stimulants, you can see some changes in behavior very quickly—even with the very first dose. Other types of medications typically take longer to start working. Antidepressants, for example, may require up to three weeks before effects are noticeable. However, with all of these medications, you should see definite changes within a couple of months.

What should I do if the medication isn't working?

About 25 percent of patients don't respond to the initial medication, or have too much trouble with side effects to stay on it. But there's good news: Patients often do well with another medication of the same type. So, for example, if Ritalin isn't helping your child, ask your doctor to consider switching him or her to Adderall or Dexedrine, and vice versa. If the stimulants don't work, ask the doctor to consider other classes of drugs instead. Also, combinations might work where single medications don't.

If medication isn't making a difference after a reasonable period of time, there's no reason to continue the same treatment regimen in the hope that it will eventually improve. Schedule an appointment with your child's physician to look at how the treatment should be modified.

Here's what you and the doctor should consider:

- The medication—another drug or class of drugs may work better.
- The dosage—if you're not seeing improvement, the dosage may need to be increased or the timing of the doses changed; if side effects are a problem, consider reducing the dosage, either temporarily or permanently.
- The diagnosis—if medication isn't proving effective, take another look at the diagnosis. Your child may have an ADHD mimicker—a different condition whose symptoms resemble ADHD.

- Comorbid disorders—as we've seen, problems such as learning disorders or anxiety often go hand in hand with ADHD. If, for example, your child has a comorbid learning disorder, you won't see much progress if you're only treating the ADHD. That doesn't mean you should stop treating the ADHD and focus only on the LD; you need to treat both.

Does medication really help my child get better grades in school?

While it's clear that medication has a powerful effect on classroom *behavior*, some researchers have questioned whether they improve *learning* as well. In other words, does medication simply help ADHD children be less disruptive in class, or does it actually improve their performance on things like book reports and math exercises? That's an important distinction, because it raises the issue of whether medication primarily benefits the child or the teacher.

While there are conflicting studies on this issue, the bulk of the evidence suggests that medication does in fact improve both behavior and academic performance. For example, a 1993 study published in the *Journal of the American Academy of Child and Adolescent Psychiatry* looked at specific areas of academic performance and found that medication helped about 75 percent of ADHD children improve to the point that their performance was essentially the same as that of non-ADHD children.

Can medication interfere *with learning?*

Yes, it can—which is why it's so important to monitor closely the child's school performance after medication begins. For example, in some cases stimulants cause children to become isolated and withdrawn. This may make it hard for a child to set priorities and move from task to task. These effects seem to be dose related, so the way to manage them is by reducing the dosage or trying a different medication.

The dosage my child is using doesn't control her ADHD all the time. Does it need to be increased?

Inconsistent control is usually a matter of when it's given, not the size of the dosage. For example, Ritalin's clinical effects may last as little as two hours, so even the standard twice-a-day regimen creates peaks and valleys of control throughout the day. Longer-acting Dexedrine often gives better results, but with any medication you may see variability.

That's why it's important to tailor the dosage schedule for your child's individual circumstances. For example, one common problem comes up with children who have a long bus ride to school. If they take their Ritalin with breakfast, they'll be fine on the bus, but the medication may start wearing off in first or second period, and the period before a second dose at lunchtime will be a complete loss. If the child can be relied on to take his medication, I often suggest that he take it when he gets off the bus at school, so that the peak effects will occur when they're most needed.

How will the doctor determine the right dose for my child?

Mostly by clinical experience, along with some degree of trial and error.

Because people respond so differently and unpredictably to ADHD medications, it's difficult to say up front what the optimal dose should be for any given patient. In most cases, the initial dose should be at the low end of the range and then gradually adjusted upward to achieve the best response— an approach known as *titration.* Titration takes more work and a longer observation time than simply writing a "standard" dose. You have to wait to see the effects and possibly return to the doctor for several follow-up visits until the dose is right. But it allows the doctor to find the lowest dose that still produces the desired effects, thus reducing the risk of side effects.

How do you know when the dose is high enough?

A basic rule of thumb is to use the lowest dosage that produces an adequate response.

"Adequate" is, of course, often in the eye of the beholder. However, keep in mind that more isn't necessarily better. With higher doses, of course, the risk of side effects increases. But there's another, less obvious reason to keep the dosages low. Studies show that too high doses begin to interfere with the ability to do very complex and memory-intensive tasks, even though they control the social and hyperactive components of ADHD. Thus, while the child's classroom *behavior* seems terrific, the actual academic *performance* isn't at its full potential. In other words, the dose that's best at controlling behavior isn't necessarily the best at promoting learning. Lower doses can control behavior without interfering with higher-level processing.

Should the dosage be set based on weight?

Not necessarily—at least not for the stimulants. Weight is a starting point for calculating dosage, but not the whole answer. That's why two patients who weigh the same may end up with very different dosages.

For many medications, dosages are calculated based on body weight, so that a child weighing 50 pounds would receive one third the dose of a man weighing 150. But several studies of stimulants suggest that body weight doesn't always make a difference. For example, one study looked at how well different doses of Ritalin controlled symptoms of ADHD in a large group of children. When researchers looked at the dosages in terms of *body weight,* there was no clear pattern of which doses were most effective. But when they ignored body weight and simply looked at the dosages, the results were dramatic: The optimal dose was usually between 10 and 15 mg, regardless of the child's size.

Of course, that doesn't mean that every child will do best at this dosage, but it does suggest a good starting point.

This same general rule holds true for Dexedrine or other medications that we use to treat ADHD. In the final analysis, we are not treating a weight, but a person.

Should the dosage increase as my child grows?

Yes. Dosage will usually increase over time as the child grows through adolescence. It's important not to fall behind in the dosing. If the child outgrows the dose, she'll begin to lose her focus, and the symptoms of ADHD will re-establish themselves—often so gradually that you won't realize there's a problem at first. It's always preferable to head off these problems rather than trying to undo damage caused by loss of focus.

Are the effects of Dexedrine, Adderall and Ritalin the same?

No. Although all of these stimulants address problems of attention and focus, they're not completely interchangeable.

In about 70 percent of patients, they have similar effects. But other patients may respond to one of these drugs and not the others, or they may have unacceptable side effects with one and not another.

What's more, each drug has a "personality" in terms of how it affects the patients. In some, Ritalin acts like blinders on a horse, keeping them highly focused. It's almost as if Ritalin tells you, "You *will* pay attention." That can be useful, but the downside is that it leaves some patients feeling "flat," lacking zest. Parents sometimes tell me that their child seems "sad" on Ritalin, but it's not really sadness; it's more like their spirits are dampened. They don't feel quite themselves. That's one reason why many adolescents don't like to take Ritalin.

I've found that Dexedrine and Adderall often produce a

more "natural" response in patients. Instead of forcing you to pay attention, it permits you to pay attention. Patients may not get the same tight focus as they do on Ritalin, but they're looser and more spontaneous.

However, Dexedrine and Adderall aren't tolerated by everyone. They don't provide the same degree of control over behavior. Also, in some patients they can produce an edginess and anger—sort of the flip side of the flatness we sometimes see in Ritalin.

The upshot is that there's no ideal treatment for everyone. For some patients, Ritalin is clearly the drug of choice; for others, it's Dexedrine or Adderall. The goal of treatment isn't to impose a one-size-fits-all approach, but to find out what's best for the individual.

What should I do if my child gets the wrong dose?

If you *miss* a dose, there's really nothing to worry about. Just give the next dose when it's scheduled. Don't double up to "make up" for the missed dose.

If you accidentally give your child too much medication, call your doctor. A double dose may cause short-term problems such as irritability, loss of appetite, and sleep difficulties. It's not likely to cause any long-term harm, but check with your doctor or pharmacist just to be sure. A major overdose— for example, if a younger sibling accidentally gets into the medication—can be much more serious. Call your doctor, your local Poison Control Center, or 911 *immediately*.

CHAPTER 5

Beyond Medication

As appealing as the idea is that behavior modification and other nondrug treatments can control ADHD without medication, research hasn't supported that view. It's clear that these techniques enhance the effectiveness of medication, but when they're used alone they have little if any effect on ADHD.

To see why this is so, let's return for a moment to the analogy of nearsightedness. Imagine a child who's never been able to learn how to read. After several years, her parents finally discover that she's nearsighted, and can't see the lessons on the blackboard.

Now, there are many effective techniques to help children master reading. And this child's teacher will need to use them to help the child make up for all the lost time. But they won't do any good *until she starts wearing glasses.*

That's exactly what happens with ADHD. Medication makes it possible for these techniques to work.

Within that context, nonmedical techniques are a critical part of treatment for ADHD. And yet all too often, they're ignored or given lip service at best. There's a common misperception that medication is the "real" treatment for ADHD, and these other techniques are just some extra frills. Not so.

In fact, these treatments often make the difference between success and failure.

Unfortunately, however, nonmedical treatments are also fertile ground for pop cures and quick fixes. Children and parents alike have invested considerable time, energy, and sometimes money on ADHD treatments that have been proven *not* to work. We'll take a closer look at all these, and then explore the techniques that have proven effective in the management of ADHD.

Will reducing the amount of sugar in my child's diet reduce his hyperactivity?

If you restrict your child's sugar intake, your dentist will love you. But it probably won't have any effect on ADHD symptoms.

The presumed link between sweets and hyperactivity is one of the most enduring myths about ADHD. On the whole, children in developed countries do get too much fat and sugar in their diets, and childhood obesity is at epidemic proportions. And poor nutrition can certainly interfere with learning, whether a child has ADHD or not. So I'm not suggesting that you shouldn't make every effort to have your children eat a balanced diet.

But the notion that a candy bar at lunchtime will make a child bounce off the walls in the afternoon just doesn't hold up in research studies. For example, Drs. D. W. Hoover and Richard Milich conducted controlled studies on the effects of sugar on child behavior and found "absolutely no suggestion that sugar adversely affects the performance of hyperactive children."* Another study looked at sugar, aspartame (i.e., NutraSweet), and thyroid conditions, and found that none of them affected the symptoms of ADHD.

---

*D. W. Hoover and R. Milich. "Effects of sugar ingestion expectancies on mother-child interactions." *Journal of the American Academy of Child and Adolescent Psychiatry* 1994; 22:501–15.

Do "food allergies" contribute to ADHD?

This is another theory that hasn't held up on close examination. Some years ago, a number of authors suggested that the behavioral problems associated with ADHD were caused or aggravated by allergies to chemical food additives. And, in fact, children with ADHD *are* more prone to allergies, including food allergies, for reasons that aren't clear. But there's little evidence that an additive-free diet will improve ADHD symptoms.

Is psychotherapy effective for ADHD?

Strictly speaking, ADHD is a *neurobiological* disorder, not a *psychological* one. In other words, it's a physical disorder of the brain, not a disorder of the mind. And psychotherapy or psychological counseling won't fix it.

However, therapy can play a very important role in helping patients deal with the *consequences* of ADHD. Children who have ADHD—especially when undiagnosed for a long time—often have feelings of shame, low self-esteem, inadequacy, and other psychological issues. And even after we've treated the physical part of ADHD, we still have to deal with these problems too.

Often, one of the best sources of help are others who are facing similar issues. Support groups—for example, through local chapters of C.h.A.D.D.—are good not only for moral support but also a good forum in which to share problems and solutions. (See Chapter 10 for a listing of such groups.)

I want to use as little medication as possible. Is it possible to use a stimulant only when needed instead of on a regular daily dosage?

From a medical standpoint, yes—as long as you're using a stimulant like Ritalin or Dexedrine or Adderall. You won't make ADHD worse if you skip a dose of medicine. And because these stimulants act fast, you could work out a medication schedule that controls ADHD symptoms at key times—for example, when your child needs to write a report or study for a test.

Most doctors and parents don't fine-tune the process that closely, but many of them establish "drug holidays" over weekends and school breaks.

I can certainly understand the desire to reduce the amount of medication that a child receives, but I don't think this approach is in your child's best interest over the long term. ADHD is about more than simply studying for a test or researching a report. It involves long-term issues, and these are much harder to address with an on-again, off-again dosage schedule.

For example, there are the social issues related to ADHD; in the long run, these may be more important than schoolwork, and they don't go away at the end of the school day. The same goes for the child's role in the family, her ability to play sports, and a long list of other issues.

Nor is learning confined to the times between homeroom and the dismissal bell. It could be argued that the most important lessons are the ones learned outside the classroom. And this learning is affected by ADHD just as much as academic performance is.

I try to recommend a middle ground for my patients. We use the lowest possible doses that control the symptoms of ADHD. And we *tailor* the dosage schedule to meet the child's needs. Some, for example, do fine without an after-school dose; other children need that last dose to keep from falling apart between dinner and bedtime.

ADHD patients are like snowflakes: No two are exactly alike. And no one-size-fits-all dosage schedule will work for everyone.

What nonmedical treatments are most effective?

In my view, one of the best nonmedical treatments for ADHD is the personal computer.

If we'd set out specifically to design a tool to help children with ADHD, we couldn't have come up with anything better than computers. They help in a number of ways:

- They use a variety of techniques to establish and maintain attention: bright colors, bold graphics, rapidly changing screens, great sound, and the tactile stimulation that a keyboard or mouse provides. In short, they involve *all* of the senses.
- They ask for and give continuous feedback: You have to click this, enter that, answer questions, type in commands. The keyboard clicks. Programs beep.
- Because of the way they acquire and store information, they impose organization—for example, grouping related work within folders and directories.
- Once a child learns to type, they help overcome dysgraphia—that is, the writing difficulties—which is common among people with ADHD.

Many of my patients find that bringing a laptop to school is a tremendous benefit. Of course, that's not an option for everyone, but there are less expensive options as well. For example, lower-cost electronic organizers can help with many of the organizational challenges of ADHD—and newer ones are designed so that information can be shared with a desktop computer at home. In addition, students often have access to computers in school. Even if they don't have a laptop on their desk, a computer in the resource room or a corner of the classroom can be an enormous asset for writing assignments and other schoolwork.

Best of all, there's no downside to computers. There aren't any side effects. The skills they teach will be useful for your entire life.

Is behavior modification effective for ADHD?

Based on techniques pioneered by B. F. Skinner and other behavioral psychologists, behavior modification aims at changing behaviors.

When used for ADHD, it begins by training parents and teachers to identify specific behaviors—for example, negative behaviors such as calling out in class or positive behaviors such as waiting to be called on. Then it devises systems to reward the child for positive behaviors and punish or ignore negative behaviors.

Most parents and teachers already use such techniques instinctively, and this approach isn't all that different from ordinary child rearing. But it attempts to take a more systematic and consistent approach.

A number of studies over the past two decades have shown that behavior modification isn't as effective as medication in treating ADHD.

However, an *integrated* approach, using behavioral techniques *combined* with medication, may make it possible to control ADHD with lower doses, according to a study of 107 ADHD children conducted by researchers at Johns Hopkins University.* Children in the study received either a placebo, a low dose of Ritalin (0.4 mg/kg), or a higher dose (0.8 mg/kg). In addition, half the children and their parents received training that included behavior modification techniques. The other half received no training.

As you'd expect, the researchers saw no significant improvement in the placebo group. But children receiving low-dose medications *plus* the training did much better—in fact, they did as well as children who received high doses of medication. But here was the biggest surprise: They did as well as children receiving *high* doses plus training.

The researchers speculate that when this training was attempted without medication, it simply didn't have a chance to work. But even the lower doses of medication seem to create an environment in which these techniques can take root and flourish.

---

*D. Meichenbaum, *Cognitive-Behavior Modification: An Integrative Approach.* New York: Plenum, 1977.

In this sense, you can think of ADHD like nearsightedness: If I can't see well, I probably will have trouble learning to read. But glasses won't teach me to read; they simply allow me to benefit from what's being taught. So it is with medication: It won't teach a child anything; it simply enables them to learn.

Although it's difficult to generalize from the results of a single study, the implications are twofold: An integrated approach can reduce the need for higher doses of medication (an important point, since most of the side effects are dose related), but medication must remain a cornerstone of treatment. These findings suggest that some of the 20 percent or so of ADHD children who can't tolerate standard doses of medication can benefit from lower doses when they're combined with an ongoing program that reinforces positive behavior and imparts specific skills for dealing with ADHD.

I—and virtually every other doctor treating ADHD—will go even further. It would be wonderful if all of our patients could get these additional interventions and support. Medication may control the outward symptoms of ADHD, but it's not the whole answer. It creates a "window of opportunity" that allows a person with ADHD to acquire the knowledge and skills he or she needs to succeed. It's up to us—physicians, parents, and teachers—to help children take advantage of that opportunity.

How does behavior modification work?

At its most basic level, behavior modification involves systems of rewards and punishments—reinforcers, as they're known in the fields. By managing these reinforcers, it becomes possible to change, or modify, behavior—hence the term.

A key part of behavior modification is measurement. Usually there is some form of behavior chart that's used to track how frequently a certain behavior occurs. Significantly, the focus is on behavior—acts that can be seen and evaluated—

rather than feelings or state of mind. Behavioral theory doesn't deny the importance of feelings, but it has no objective way to measure them.

Behavioral principles are fairly simple and we all use behavior modification techniques in our daily lives. But a formal behavior modification program can be quite complex, because some "reinforcers" may have unintended consequences. Any such program should be created with the help of a mental health professional who's well versed in the discipline.

That said, however, certain behavioral principles are useful in day-to-day settings. For example, in the chapter on schools we'll take a close look at the use of positive reinforcements such as praise, and why they're not used as much as they should be. For now, the key point to keep in mind is that positive reinforcement works *better* than punishment, even though punishment works *faster*.

That short-term payoff makes it tempting to use punishment as a control, even though it may create more problems than it solves in the long run. So it's important to make a *conscious, ongoing* effort to use positive reinforcement. For example, you might make up a behavior chart for yourself—tracking how often you give out praise versus criticism.

What is cognitive training and how well does it work?

Cognitive training is an approach first developed in the 1970s to manage ADHD. It's based on teaching children specific skills. For example, children are taught to control impulsive behavior by planning in advance, stopping to think before acting, making a plan and following it. To help with social difficulties, they're taught conflict-resolution skills.

Cognitive training hasn't really proved to be an effective alternative to medication. Several extensive pilot programs produced virtually no improvement in ADHD symptoms.

As reasonable as this approach sounds, it's based on the

assumption that the impulsive behavior of ADHD involves a lack of skills. But that assumption wasn't supported by later evidence showing the biological basis of the disorder.

We've tried using positive reinforcement, and it doesn't seem to work. Why not? .

As I mentioned, when you're employing behavioral modification techniques, there's a risk of unintended consequences. Something that seems as if it should be a reward turns out not to make the behavior better—or even makes it worse.

The techniques aren't to blame; it's how they're being applied. For example, here are some of the most common ways that positive reinforcement gets derailed:

Giving the reward first. "If I let you watch TV, you have to do your homework as soon as the show is over." What kid wouldn't agree to that deal? Your child isn't trying to take advantage of you; it's just that positive reinforcement doesn't work unless it comes after the behavior.

Assuming rewards have to be things. In fact, the strongest positive reinforcement you can give isn't money or a new toy. It's praise—as long as you really mean it.

Delayed gratification. The more time elapses between the behavior and the reward, the less effective that reward becomes. If you tell your child that he can earn five stickers on Friday for a week of good behavior, he'll be less motivated than if he earns one sticker every day of the week.

Setting the bar too high. You can't reinforce behavior that doesn't occur. If you decide to reward your child for completing twenty math problems at a time and she's never finished more than ten, you're setting her up for failure. Start with a goal of, say, twelve. Once she's achieved that, increase the stakes gradually. Eventually you may get to twenty—just not all at once.

Think of trained porpoises. I'm not comparing your child to a show animal, but the trainers use the same basic behavioral principles with them. And they don't teach the porpoises to do a double back flip all at once. They work up to it gradually.

Not using enough. Some parents fear they'll "spoil" a child with too much positive reinforcement, or that the technique will lose its punch. But I can't recall ever seeing a patient suffering from an overdose of praise—as long as it's genuine. The problem with flattery isn't that it's repeated, but that it's disbelieved. Think of positive reinforcement not so much as a reward as a guidepost—it helps your child know when he's on the right path. And especially for a child with ADHD, you need to set out as many of those guideposts as possible.

Not enough variety. To keep reinforcers fresh, don't use the same ones all the time. Sometimes it can be a trip to the park or playing a game; other times it can be a hug or a bedtime story. Mix them up.

Giving praise too consistently. While it's important to give lots of praise, there's also a risk in giving reinforcement too consistently. If you reward a desired behavior every single time it happens, what happens when you stop? The behavior will stop occurring soon afterward.

Studies show that the best reinforcement schedules are random: You may get a reward often, but you're never quite sure when. If you think about how people buy lottery tickets, you can see this principle in action: People may win several hundred dollars one week, and then go for months or years before winning again. They keep buying tickets (i.e., engaging in the desired behavior) because they don't know when the next reinforcement will come.

Along the same lines, it's not always a good idea to announce what the reward will be beforehand—or even that there will *be* a reward. If you're using a formal behavior modification program you may need to be explicit in the beginning, just to get the ball rolling. But over time an element of uncertainty makes the behavior more likely to "stick"—that is, to become a permanent behavior change.

Some of this sounds counterintuitive. It may be useful to

remember this important fact: When you give a reward, you're not really reinforcing the behavior that just occurred. It's history, and nothing you do after the fact is going to affect it. Reinforcement is really aimed at *future* behavior.

With all this emphasis on positive behavior, are you saying we shouldn't punish our child if he does something wrong?

I'm not saying that. Punishment—for example, the loss of privileges—has its place, especially in ADHD. But it's only part of the equation.

Punishment is good for reducing *negative* behaviors—and there's plenty of negative behavior to reduce. But positive reinforcement fills in the rest of the ledger, by promoting *positive* behaviors. Both are necessary.

What kinds of punishment are appropriate?

Generally, time-out strategies work best, especially for young children. Loss of privileges is also effective.

But punishments that promote shame, anger, or low self-esteem—such as sarcasm or physical punishment—usually do more harm than good. That's especially true for ADHD children, whose self-esteem is often low to begin with.

One yardstick you can use is "punishment with dignity." You can impose negative consequences on a child while still preserving his basic sense of self-worth. For example, one common piece of advice is to punish the behavior, not the child. I agree with that approach wholeheartedly, because it allows the child to retain his dignity.

Besides behavior modification, are there other techniques that are effective for ADHD?

Anything that makes a task more stimulating will help an ADHD stay focused and attentive.

We have covered how stimulants improve attention by

making neurotransmitters more available to brain cells. It appears that other kinds of stimulation—for example, loud noise, cold air, physical activity—trigger similar changes in the brain.

You can see evidence of that in daily life. For example, if you've been driving for hours and you're having trouble paying attention to the road, what are you likely to do? Roll down the window and let the cold air blow on your face, perhaps, or put on loud music, or stretch and yawn. We take such strategies for granted, but they raise an interesting question: Shouldn't this stimulation *distract* you even more from the task at hand? In fact, it doesn't. It helps you concentrate.

Or consider how people work under pressure. An impending deadline, the risk of failure, intense competition—all of these provide stimulation that can produce an intense degree of focus.

These examples suggest a whole new way of looking at the typical kinds of behavior that occur in ADHD. We usually view the wiggling and wandering, the acting out and running around as symptoms of inattention. In fact, they may be the body's effort to increase stimulation to *combat* inattention—just like rolling down the car window or turning on loud music.

If that view is correct—and it's still only a theory—then it may make more sense to work *with* these self-stimulating efforts rather than try to suppress them.

What can we do to help increase stimulation for our child?

Many parents and teachers report that nondrug stimulation *does* help their ADHD children focus better. Here are some general strategies:

Risk. It's probably no accident that many people with ADHD seem to be risk takers; the stimulation probably helps them focus. By incorporating some element of risk into tasks, you may be able to help them stay focused. (Beware, though, if a comorbid anxiety disorder is present; a perceived risk may worsen the anxiety.)

For example, consider making homework into a contest: "Do your homework while I wash these dishes. Whoever finishes first, wins." (Note that you don't have to offer a prize for winning. It's the competition, not the reward, that provides the stimulation.) Another way to inject risk is by setting short-term deadlines: "Let's see if you can finish this page of homework in ten minutes." Competitive teams and games are other ways to make tasks more stimulating.

Measurable goals. Closely related to the idea of contests is the importance of having *measurable* goals. Again, this is true for anyone: At work, are you more focused on a goal of "doing a good job" or "getting Project X done on time"?

Charting helps focus performance and progress: "Last week you finished ten problems in ten minutes. Let's see if you can beat the record." When you're using charts, it's better to chart outcomes rather than behavior. It's more objective and gives the child more control over *how* she will meet the goal. For example, "time spent on-task" is harder to measure than "put my socks in the hamper."

Also, goals that are just a little bit in the future are more stimulating than longer-term goals. If Project X is due next Thursday, it probably commands more attention than Project Y that's due in three months—even if Project Y is intrinsically more important and interesting.

(That's why, incidentally, many children with ADHD often have a slump in the middle of the school year. At the beginning of the year, the novelty of the new class and teacher provide stimulation. And when the end of the year comes into sight, it provides a focus that helps the child move forward.)

Physical stimulation. A quiet, comfortable place to work may be best for most children with ADHD, but not all of them. For example, one child worked best in the kitchen because she needed someone to help her stay focused. Others may think better while they're pacing or doodling; teachers shouldn't necessarily assume that such behavior means the child isn't paying attention.

Movement. Obviously, too much physical activity is disruptive. But too little can be a problem, too. For example, a teacher shouldn't assume that a child who's squirming in his seat or drumming his fingers isn't paying attention. That may be his *way* of paying attention.

This points up a common mistake in managing ADHD: focusing too much on the "means" rather than the "ends." Take the classroom, for example: The goal of treatment isn't for the child to sit still; it's for the child to learn. If the child finds it easier to pay attention by doodling on a scratch pad, looking at the ceiling or standing on one foot next to his desk—and she isn't disrupting the class—then why not?

Interests. We're all more stimulated by things that are relevant to ourselves and our interests. (That's why people read local newspapers.) As a parent, you know your child's hot buttons better than anyone. Use that universal principle to your advantage.

Say your child has an interest in fashion design and she's studying English history. There's nothing wrong in encouraging her to explore the role of fashion in Elizabethan times. By relating schoolwork to a child's interest, you can make the subject more relevant and stimulating.

Variety. It's more stimulating than the same old thing. Earlier we talked about the importance of routines and structure for people with ADHD, as a way of helping them organize themselves. But routine doesn't mean monotony. *Within* this basic organizational scheme, there are many opportunities to provide variety. Things as simple as a teacher moving around the room, talking louder or softer, faster or slower—all help keep the level of stimulation higher. The same is true in other settings—for example, if you're on a long car trip with the kids, try rotating the seating after each rest stop.

Problem solving. Coming up with a solution is more stimulating than simply absorbing facts, and more learning takes place. For example, instead of asking a child to memorize a list of spelling words, you can make the words "clues" that need to be solved to find the answer to a puzzle. A provocative discussion topic also challenges students to think and concentrate. Instead of teaching who won the Civil War, challenge students to think of what the South could have done to win.

Music. As odd as it sounds, many ADHD children have better success doing their homework with the music blaring (again, think of the driver-fatigue analogy). This certainly isn't a strategy that I'd advocate for every child with ADHD, but before you forbid the radio during homework time, take a look at whether your child actually gets her homework done more quickly and accurately with the radio on.

The best results come when a child has a repertoire of these methods to increase stimulation. That way, if one isn't working, he can try another. And while many children use such strategies unconsciously, it's good for the child to be able to *identify* these strategies so that he can call on them when needed. Work with your child and his teacher to come up with a variety of stimulation strategies that are appropriate and nondisruptive.

CHAPTER 6

ADHD and Other Problems

One of the most significant developments recently in the treatment of ADHD is the recognition of the role of *comorbid* disorders—other conditions that often accompany ADHD. These combinations occur more commonly than most people think, and they help explain why some cases of ADHD are resistant to treatment. When ADHD is complicated by other problems such as depression or learning disorders, standard treatment isn't enough; to be effective, treatment must address the accompanying disorder as well.

What other conditions are associated with ADHD?

A variety of behavioral disorders are more common among children with ADHD than those without it. The most common are learning disabilities (such as dyslexia), mood disorders (especially depression), anxiety, and oppositional and conduct disorders.

How prevalent are these related disorders?

Because of the complex interactions among these various disorders, researchers come up with different estimates of how much overlap there is (see the list that follows). But the most recent studies suggest that about half of all children with ADHD also have, or will develop, one of these comorbid conditions.

In a group of 140 children with ADHD, researcher Joseph Biederman found that this many *also* had other conditions:*

Oppositional defiant disorder	50%
Anxiety disorder	33%
Learning disability (dyslexia)	30%
Major depression	20%
Conduct disorder	20%

We in the field have only recently begun to understand the magnitude of this problem, and it underscores more than ever the need to create a treatment program specifically tailored to the child's needs. Treating ADHD isn't like treating an ear infection, where you make the diagnosis, write the prescription, and instruct the parents to call you if the child doesn't get better in a few days.

Rather, in about half the cases doctors must manage multiple disorders. It's as if half of the children who showed up at the doctor's office with ear infections also had asthma, or heart problems, or poor eyesight. If the doctor focuses only on the ear infection because that's what the presenting complaint is, he or she is going to miss a lot of diagnoses.

So it is with ADHD. When a child is referred to the doctor because the school or parents think she has ADHD, it's a signal to assess the child for other, related disorders as well.

If these comorbid conditions are so common, why didn't my doctor notice them?

Diagnosing comorbid conditions can get very tricky. Many of the symptoms overlap—for example, depression can cause

---

*Joseph Biederman, unpublished results.

inattention, and the difficulties that ADHD causes can make you feel depressed. As a result, doctors often run into a chicken-and-egg problem when making these diagnoses: Is it depression that looks like ADHD? ADHD that's mimicking depression? Or are there two separate conditions coexisting?

Even the experts aren't sure where to draw the line. Various studies report different rates of comorbidity. But all of them show there's significant overlap between ADHD and certain other conditions.

For any child with ADHD, it's a good idea to have a child psychiatrist conduct periodic assessments to screen for comorbid conditions. A specialist should be reviewing your child's case every six months to a year to be sure everything's on track, and that's a good opportunity to assess the child for comorbid conditions.

Of course, if there's a problem, you shouldn't wait that long. In most cases, your gut instincts are the best indicator. If everything's going well, great. But if you have an uneasy feeling that things aren't getting better—or are actually getting worse—it's probably time to seek an outside opinion.

Why do these conditions seem to go hand in hand with ADHD?

Nobody really knows for sure. One possible explanation is that these conditions involve some of the same chemical processes and neurological pathways in the brain. For example, depression and ADHD are both associated with neurotransmitter imbalances. Another possibility is that one condition may be triggered or worsened by an accompanying disorder. As we saw above, for example, untreated ADHD can lead to social isolation, academic underachievement, and other problems that put one at risk for substance abuse and conduct disorder. Or it may work the other way: We may find that a child who had mild or borderline ADHD may develop more severe attentional problems as a result of depression or anxiety disorders.

How are comorbid conditions treated when ADHD is present?

In most cases, they're treated the same way as if they stood alone. Except for, perhaps, some cases of depression, there's no single combination treatment.

So once the diagnosis of these other conditions is established, your doctor will likely recommend two simultaneous, but separate, courses of treatment.

Do treatments for comorbid conditions interfere with the treatment of ADHD?

Generally, no. When used properly, treatments for the most common comorbid conditions neither affect nor are affected by ADHD treatments. In fact, treating ADHD and the comorbid disorder is the only way to produce a complete success. When we treat one but overlook the other, we're often left with a lingering sense that something is still wrong. For example, treating ADHD when there's a hidden comorbid disorder may indeed yield some improvement, but not the full effect that we expect to see.

What warning signs of anxiety should I look for?

Here are some of the most common:

- Difficulty making up one's mind
- Feelings of fear and nervousness
- Physical symptoms such as heart palpitations, sweating, etc.
- Worrying over seemingly insignificant things
- Short temper
- Feelings of inadequacy or not being liked
- Feelings of isolation
- Stomachaches
- Nightmares
- Difficulty concentrating
- Physical restlessness, fidgeting
- Feelings of numbness; hot flashes
- Feelings of dread

How are anxiety disorders treated?

The philosophy we follow for treating depression holds true for anxiety and other comorbid conditions as well: Instead of trying to find a one-size-fits-all treatment, it's best to find the optimal approach for *each* condition and treat accordingly.

There are many medication options for treating anxiety, and treatment depends on individual circumstances. I often prescribe beta blockers such as Inderal for anxiety. These medications, which are often used to treat heart conditions, effectively control anxiety symptoms, without the mind-altering properties that we see with drugs such as Valium and Xanax. What's more, beta blockers have virtually no potential for abuse or addiction.

Like so many of the drugs we've been discussing, beta blockers work by affecting the interaction between cells and neurotransmitters. They block receptors on the cell known as "beta receptors," which are sensitive to the neurotransmitter epinephrine. By blocking these receptors, the drug makes the cells in the brain (as well as the heart and elsewhere in the body) less sensitive to epinephrine's effects. That, in turn, blunts the symptoms of anxiety, such as sweaty palms, rapid shallow breathing, palpitations, and the like.

A caution, however: As with all comorbid conditions, it's important to figure out what's really going on first, before treatment for anxiety begins. For example, if the anxiety is situational (whether because of ADHD-related problems or other issues confronting the patient), you can't simply medicate it away. The treatment plan must include strategies to address these underlying issues. For example, if a child is experiencing debilitating anxiety because of unrealistic expectations in school, we need to look at modifying the environment—for example by implementing some of the school-related strategies we will discuss in Chapter 7.

The child and/or parents may also have to take a hard look at their expectations. If a student is struggling to get C's in high school but feels she *must* get into Stanford or Yale, she's setting herself up for failure and its consequences (such as anxiety or depression). Not every student gets into Stanford and Yale. Not every student should. And among those who do, some would have been better off if they hadn't.

One of the gifts of ADHD is that it teaches people early in their lives that there isn't one single path to fulfillment. Just as there's no one best way to do homework, there's no one best way to live one's life. Some of the most successful and fulfilled people I know have ADHD. But many of them arrived at this success in unorthodox ways. If we can teach ADHD children one lesson, it should be this one.

What are the warning signs of obsessive-compulsive disorder?

OCD usually shows itself in a rigidity of behavior—for example, behavioral routines. Here are some signs that may alert you to the possibility of OCD:

- Rigid patterns of behavior; for example, adhering to elaborate routines and rituals of behavior
- A fixation on certain ideas, images, or impulses, often for no apparent reason
- Constant worry that bad things will happen because of something one did or failed to do (such as locking the door)
- Fear of losing things
- Perfectionism
- Difficulty throwing things away; for example, saving scraps of paper

How is obsessive-compulsive disorder treated?

OCD is usually treated with selective serotonin-reuptake inhibitor antidepressants such as Tofranil, Paxil, Prozac, or Luvox—not because the person is depressed, but because OCD seems to involve related chemical pathways in the brain.

In comorbid cases, antidepressants may be effective for both the OCD and ADHD. Since they're first-line treatment for OCD, it often makes sense to begin these patients on antidepressants alone, reserving stimulants for those patients whose ADHD isn't adequately controlled.

There are a number of other treatments for OCD that may be used instead of, or in addition to, antidepressants. For example, behavioral treatments are aimed at reducing compulsive *behaviors*, although they generally don't help with obsessive *thinking*.

What are the warning signs of learning disabilities?

Learning disabilities come in lots of varieties, some more obvious than others. Most are identified in the schools. Experienced teachers are usually quick to spot students who are having difficulty learning.

There is a risk, however, that these disabilities will be overlooked in a child who's been diagnosed with ADHD. Teachers may assume that whatever difficulties the child is experiencing are due to the ADHD, when in fact there's a comorbid learning disability that must be addressed. The best way to flag these problems is to look at whether academic problems persist even after ADHD treatment begins. Although it may take some time to unlearn old study habits and acquire new ones, you should see some evidence of academic improvement very quickly with stimulant treatment (more slowly with the antidepressants).

If you don't see improvement, consider two possibilities: Either the medication isn't as effective as it should be against the symptoms of ADHD, or other factors are interfering with learning.

You should be especially watchful for comorbid learning disabilities when ADHD medication improves behavior but not schoolwork. Likewise, if there's evidence that the medication is improving attention in other situations (such as sports and social interactions) but having little effect on academic performance, ask the school to assess your child for learning disabilities. Careful evaluation is needed not only to determine whether a learning disability is present but also to diagnose accurately the specific type of disability.

How are learning disabilities treated?

Unlike ADHD, learning disabilities such as dyslexia can't be treated with medication. They require the help of a trained learning specialist. The good news is that this remediation is usually extraordinarily successful. (Interestingly, when you take a close look at people who've successfully "overcome" dyslexia, you find that the basic decoding issues are still there; they develop compensatory skills that allow them to "work around" the disability. But if, for example, you ask them to read aloud, you can tell that the dyslexia is still there. Adults with dyslexia rarely like Scrabble or other word games, because they have difficulty visualizing the words.)

Before treatment begins, however, it's vitally important to be sure just what's going on. Many children who've been diagnosed late with ADHD have missed some learning along the way because of their attentional difficulties. Their education is kind of like Swiss cheese: Parts of it are solid, but then you run across a big empty hole where, say, you'd expect to find the rules for long division or spelling of state capitals. These gaps are learning *deficiencies*, not learning *disabilities*. Filling them in is pretty straightforward once you've identified them, and they don't require a learning specialist. A good teacher or tutor can help a child make up this lost ground.

Learning disabilities, on the other hand, involve the way we acquire and process information. So, for example, dyslexia is a problem with decoding letters and words on a page; dyscalcia is a similar difficulty with numbers. Tutors can't help with these kinds of problems; you need the specialized assistance that a learning specialist can provide. In fact, tutors and homework helpers may actually do such children a disservice, by allowing them to get through homework without mastering skills such as decoding words.

What warning signs of depression should I look for?

Depression is surprisingly easy to overlook. Often it comes on gradually, and the signs may be subtle. They may be mistaken for the occasional case of the blues or sadness that we all experience.

Here are some signs to watch for:

- A lingering sense of sadness, loss, or hopelessness
- Crying, especially for no apparent reason
- Sense of dread
- Sense of failure, of letting others down
- Loss of appetite
- Changes in sleep patterns, especially insomnia
- Withdrawal, noncommunicativeness
- Loss of interest in friends or activities
- A decline in school performance
- Recent event or events representing significant loss (for example, death of a loved one, school failure, divorce, older sibling moving away, etc.)
- Physical ailments, such as aches and pains, stomachaches, headaches

How is depression treated?

We've already met some of the medications used for depression. In some cases of comorbid depression and ADHD, drugs such as Effexor or Wellbutrin offer "one-stop shopping"—a single medication that treats both conditions.

However, that's not always the best option. As we've seen, antidepressants are generally regarded as a second-line treatment for ADHD: They're a good alternative for people who don't respond to or can't tolerate stimulants. But when stimulants can be used, they usually work better.

Until just a few years ago, the tricyclic types of antidepressants were the treatment of choice for depression. But they have some of the same drawbacks for depression as for ADHD: They take a long time to start working and in some patients they cause distressing side effects.

The newest class of antidepressants, the selective serotonin reuptake inhibitors (SSRI), are quickly emerging as the treatment of choice for depression. These drugs, which include Prozac, Zoloft, and Paxil, work in that same place between the synapses where all the action is in both depression and ADHD (see page 31). Where ADHD seems to be caused by deficiencies in the norepinephrine and dopaminergic systems, depression appears to be related to similar deficiencies in serotonin. SSRIs block the ability of neurons to reabsorb serotonin. That leaves more of it available within the synapse, which improves the symptoms of depression.

Despite recent criticisms of Prozac in the popular press, it's among the most effective and safe treatments for clinical depression. (The question of whether it's being prescribed for people who don't really have depression is another issue.) And even though it's popularly viewed as an "adult" drug, in my practice I've found it to be safe and effective for children suffering from depression as well.

But as I've mentioned, SSRIs have no effect on attention, so when we use them in comorbid ADHD and depression we usually combine them with stimulants. Another alternative is to use Wellbutrin or Effexor, a new medication that blocks the reuptake of both serotonin *and* norepinephrine, another neurotransmitter. Through their action on norepinephrine, these drugs often have a positive effect on attention.

What are the warning signs of oppositional-defiant disorder?

Oppositional-defiant disorder (ODD) is a somewhat vague and elastic term. Essentially, it includes what most of us would call acting out or defiant behavior—the child who won't follow the class rules, refuses to do his homework (as opposed to being unable to do it), won't go to bed without a fight, throws his food across the room when he doesn't like it, and so on.

What makes this different from run-of-the-mill discipline problems is a pattern of consistency over a period of time, as well as the severity of the behavior. Every child occasionally gets into conflicts with parents, teachers, and friends. Some are more argumentative than others by virtue of their personality (or role models). But oppositional-defiant disorder is more pervasive, leading to a pattern of significant problems: for example, school suspensions, fights, poor grades, social isolation, and so on.

There's considerable debate in the psychiatric community over whether ODD is a "real" disorder, since plenty of normal kids exhibit some of these behaviors at times. And there's no clear line separating it from normal behavior. It's more of a continuum.

In the case of ADHD, I'm not sure it makes much sense to view oppositional behavior as a separate, comorbid disorder. Almost always, it's part and parcel of ADHD.

In my view, when children with ADHD exhibit these kinds of behaviors, they're attempting to establish control over their lives. An ADHD child's world often seems to be an endless string of overwhelming, confusing, and seemingly arbitrary demands. So when the teacher says "left" and the ADHD child replies "right," she is not just being contrary; she is trying to set her own rules to make sense of things. If the child feels she cannot win in our world, she'll oppose our rules and choose her own as a way of protecting her fragile sense of self. And as treatment helps the child feel more in control, we usually see these sorts of behaviors disappear all on their own.

My child is constantly getting into arguments with his teacher. Does he have ODD?

Not unless this behavior is part of a broader pattern of difficulties. You can't make a clinical judgment just on the basis of one or two symptoms; you need to look at them in context. It may be a sign of ODD, or it may just be a matter of personality or the normal adjustments of growing up.

How is oppositional behavior treated?

Usually, we find that it goes away all by itself when we treat the ADHD. (In this respect, it's different from most other comorbid disorders.) If it doesn't, that usually tells us that there's something else going on that we've overlooked, so we go back and reassess the diagnosis.

What are the warning signs of substance abuse?

It seems that at least some people with ADHD—especially those whose condition is undiagnosed and untreated—start using drugs in an attempt to self-medicate. Either they use drugs that help them focus, or drugs that help them avoid. The two most widely abused drugs among people with ADHD are cocaine, which is a tremendously focusing drug, and marijuana, whose primary effect is to help people withdraw from unpleasant or uncomfortable situations.

Interestingly, it seems that many people with ADHD take cocaine to feel normal. In a group of cocaine users, most will go out and party. The one who goes home and reads a book is the one with ADHD. Recent brain-imaging studies on ADHD show that the part of the brain that plays a key role in ADHD—a region known as the caudate nucleus—is the very same part of the brain that's affected by cocaine.

Many parents assume they'll know if their kid is taking drugs. Don't count on it. The signs may be more subtle than a roach left in the ashtray. Here are some common signs to look for:

- Unexplained and unpredictable changes in behavior (for example, a sudden rise in school detentions)
- New friends (caution: they won't necessarily look like drug dealers)

- A decline in performance at school or work
- Secretive or furtive behavior
- Money problems—for example, a teenager who suddenly wants to work longer hours in a part-time job; money missing from around the house, etc.

If there's a suspicion of drug use, your child's doctor can perform a urine test to confirm it.

How is substance abuse treated?

As with other oppositional behaviors, we often see substance abuse problems get better all on their own once we treat the ADHD, because the reasons for it go away.

For example, I had a patient, a teenager, who told me he got stoned on pot before every class. Since the high from marijuana typically lasts several hours, I asked him why he felt the need to light up so frequently. He told me, "Because it's so painful to be in class, I don't want to take *any* chances. I want to make sure my head is somewhere else."

Six months later, after we'd started treatment for ADHD, I asked him if he was still getting stoned before every class. He looked at me as if I were crazy. "Stoned?" he asked. "How could I get my work done in school if I got stoned?"

Even with cocaine, which has a well-deserved reputation as one of the most addictive drugs known, we often see the same thing: With proper treatment, the person with ADHD tends to lose interest in using cocaine.

Sometimes—especially when the drug abuse has been going on for a long time—it isn't that easy. Sometimes the child has a long-standing relationship with a peer group that perpetuates drug use. Sometimes it's simply become an integral part of his daily lifestyle and sense of himself. In such cases, more intensive therapy may be needed—for example, a twelve-step program. In addition to these interventions, we also look at individual, group and family therapy.

While we're on the subject of twelve-step programs, let me offer one caveat: Occasionally—not often—a program will counsel a participant that they shouldn't be taking Ritalin or Dexedrine because these drugs have abuse potential. Usually this attitude comes out of ignorance of how these drugs are used in the treatment of ADHD, and when we show that, *among people with ADHD,* the risk of abuse is virtually nonexistent, that usually settles the issue. In the unlikely event that it doesn't, there are two options: Find a different twelve-step program, or use a different medication, such as an antidepressant, that will not raise the "abuse" issue. However, my view is that if a patient's doing well otherwise with stimulants, I'd be reluctant to switch the medication.

But don't stimulants have a high potential for abuse?

Certainly. But interestingly, not among people with ADHD. Those with ADHD may abuse other drugs—most commonly cocaine, marijuana, or alcohol—but not stimulants. And people who do abuse stimulants almost never have ADHD.

When we think of people who abuse amphetamines, the images that usually come to mind are classic "speed freaks" and people using them as diet pills.

A more recent development, and one that may strike closer to home, is a trend among kids to inhale Ritalin as a study aid. Again, these aren't usually the ones with ADHD. But your child may get involved when their fellow students ask them for pills.

When I talk to my patients about this, I try to appeal to their own experience. If their friends think they need Ritalin to study, I say, isn't it better that they see a doctor? It may be a sign that they, too, have ADHD. And I emphasize that if they "lend" pills to friends, they're acting as their doctors, and they're morally accountable for the consequences. Stimulants, when used properly, are excellent medications. However, we must be vigilant to prevent their abuse.

What are the warning signs of conduct disorder?

Conduct disorder is a clinical term for the severe behavioral problems that most of us might refer to as delinquency: Getting in trouble with the law, antisocial behavior, dropping out of school, and the like.

There's a high rate of comorbidity between conduct disorder and ADHD, but that doesn't mean every child with ADHD is at risk for developing the disorder. Rather, it appears that in these cases, conduct disorder is the *primary* underlying disorder, and the attentional problems are a consequence of it.

In other words, you can think of two separate groups: The very large pool of people who have primary ADHD, and a much smaller group that's prone to conduct disorder, and whose ADHD symptoms are part and parcel of the disorder. Even though the attentional issues look similar, these are very different populations.

Nonetheless, ADHD symptoms often serve as an early warning of conduct disorder, and it's something we look for during the initial evaluation.

My child gets in fights at school. Is this conduct disorder?

In and of itself, no. Conduct disorder is more than ordinary discipline problems. It's practically a way of life, and it includes severe problems in almost every aspect of one's life. A child with true conduct disorder is very different from a child with ADHD; they lack the air of innocence and "sweetness" that we usually see in children with ADHD.

Unfortunately, parents are often in the worst position to identify these problems. On the one hand, you may fear that every after-school detention is the beginning of a long decline into delinquency. On the other hand, you may miss some valid warning signs because you're so close to the situation. But by and large, if your child has conduct disorder you'll probably know there's a problem. It may not be identified as such, but there are usually a lot of danger signs.

How is conduct disorder treated?

Conduct disorder requires intensive and ongoing therapy. It's not something that can be managed on your own, or with a pill and occasional visit to the pediatrician's office. Treatment is individualized, and may include individual counseling, group therapy, family therapy, and, in many cases, a special treatment program for kids in trouble.

One of the biggest problems in treating conduct disorder is that the problems are usually quite severe by the time the condition is diagnosed and treatment begins. A diagnosis of ADHD can serve as an early warning system. Knowing that ADHD children are at risk for this disorder, we can identify potential problems and head them off sooner, and thus more effectively.

Aren't these kids just the result of poor parenting?

No. Research tells us that conduct disorder, like ADHD, has a strong genetic basis. It runs in families—and not because those families are dysfunctional. (In fact, the dysfunction is probably a *consequence*, not a *cause*, of the disorder.) Of course, people who have conduct disorder themselves generally don't make good parents, but even when we factor this in, the evidence strongly suggests an underlying neurobiological basis for this disorder.

Indeed, there's growing evidence that most of the comorbid disorders are, like ADHD, rooted in biology much more than upbringing.

CHAPTER 7

ADHD in School

The school environment—with its schedules and assignments, its long stretches of desk work, its emphasis on writing—all too often becomes a battleground to the child with ADHD.

The battle of the classroom can't be won with medication alone. It's only the initial building block. Study after study shows that medication alone doesn't improve academic achievement.

Medication doesn't teach anything; it simply removes a major barrier to learning. If the classroom environment doesn't support the specific needs of the child with ADHD, most of the benefits of medication will be wasted.

Fortunately, an ADHD-friendly learning environment is good for all students. ADHD children will likely need more individual attention in and out of the classroom, but some of the organizational strategies are broadly applicable and beneficial. And most of them are simple, quick to implement, and involve little or no added expense.

What steps should my child's teacher and school take to help my child succeed in the classroom?

Here are some of the supports that schools and teachers should consider for children with ADHD. Your child may not need all of these supports, but discuss them with the teacher and administration:

1. Perhaps most important, modify assignments. Children with ADHD take far longer to complete in-class and homework assignments, especially those involving written work. So a workload that would be fine for a typical student may be overwhelming to a child with ADHD. It's not "cheating" to modify the assignments, any more than it would be "cheating" to make accommodations for a child with a physical or visual impairment.

The purpose of an assignment should be to help a child develop or demonstrate mastery over the material, not to complete a certain number of problems in a certain amount of time. And there's more than one way to arrive at that goal. When the assignments are too long or intensive, the child is set up for frustration and failure, and likely to feel alienated from the learning process. That's a big price to pay for the sake of a few division problems.

Because writing is often the most difficult part of school for a child with ADHD, the teacher might consider having the child answer questions orally or dictate some of his or her homework. It's even better if the child can learn to type papers on a computer (see page 67).

The teacher should limit homework assignments to what is critical and necessary. For example, the teacher might have the child complete only the even-numbered problems.

Children with ADHD need more time to finish work and tests, especially those that require a lot of writing. So untimed tests are often useful. And the child should be given the opportunity to complete unfinished classwork at home.

2. Provide support to help your child stay on task. This may involve one-on-one supervision during certain activities by an aide or specialist. It may simply mean that the teacher needs to watch for inattentiveness and call on your child more often to keep him or her focused on the material. It may mean some out-of-class tutoring or enrichment.

The physical environment is important, too. One of the most basic steps is to move the child to a desk at the front of the class. That keeps him or her more focused on the teacher and the blackboard. It also means the child is less likely to be distracted by what the other children are doing. Placing a child with ADHD next to a student who is well organized is also helpful. Some schools set aside a quiet space in one part of the classroom where a child can complete an assignment.

3. Provide organizational tools and assistance. The teacher should make sure that your child is recording assignments properly and keeping his or her materials organized. Children with ADHD need extra organizational time between classes and when they're getting their work ready to take home. Look for tools and materials that help the child stay organized—for example, such children will do better taking notes in a spiral ring notebook than on looseleaf paper. And one multisection notebook for all notes is probably better than smaller separate notebooks for each class—it's easier to keep track of. Organizers may also be helpful, as long as they're not too complicated. And ADHD children will need extra work on their study habits and organizational skills. Providing the child with a written list of assignments—either at the beginning of the week or day by day—can head off major conflicts at school and at home.

4. Above all, the school and teacher should ensure that the child's self-esteem is preserved. It may be difficult dealing with an ADHD child in the classroom, but there's no excuse for humiliating a child or singling him or her out in front of classmates. Indeed, because children with ADHD often have social difficulties, enlist the teacher's help to promote peer interaction, and to find opportunities for the child to succeed in his own eyes and the eyes of his peers.

For example, cueing is a technique that can help a child stay on task without embarrassing her. The teacher and student agree beforehand on a certain cue that the teacher will give to remind a child to pay attention—a tap on the shoulder, or a certain word. That avoids the humiliation of announcing in front of the class, "Sarah, pay attention."

What should I do if the school administration doesn't "believe" in ADHD?

Fortunately, there aren't many school administrators these days who don't acknowledge the existence of ADHD. Most of them understand implicitly what ADHD is all about, because the school has been dealing with its consequences for years. And they usually welcome the news that there may be a physical explanation, and effective treatment, for a child's learning and behavior difficulties.

However, there are doubtless still some schools whose administrators don't accept that ADHD is a "real" disease. If your child is in such a school and you have the option to send her elsewhere, consider doing so. It may be possible to change the administration's mind by presenting facts and evidence, or to bring legal pressure to bear on the school. But you may find yourself spending a lot of time and energy arguing with the administration over basic issues, energy that you may be able to put to better use elsewhere.

My child's school accepts the diagnosis, but suggests my child would be better off in another school better equipped to handle ADHD. What are my options?

This problem occurs most often in private schools.

Your child may in fact do better at another school, but this should not be a decision forced on you by a school administration that doesn't understand the nature of ADHD.

In most cases an ADHD child isn't a candidate for a special or protected learning environment. With some simple modifications and accommodations, they belong in ordinary classrooms. Like any child, a student with ADHD may do better in one school or classroom than in another. For example, they'll probably do better in a school with smaller class sizes, and worse in a school with open classrooms where numerous activities are taking place simultaneously.

But with proper and complete treatment, a child with ADHD should do fine in most classroom settings. If your child isn't doing well despite medication, you may need to see if he has a coexisting learning disability. About 40 percent of children with ADHD do, and as we saw in the previous chapter, they need different types of help than the child who has ADHD alone.

You may wish to look for another school if your child is simply not adjusting well to the school he's in. But if such a course is being urged upon you by school administrators, be sure they're acting in your child's best interest, not because they don't want to deal with children who have ADHD.

If the school is truly putting your child's interest first, its first step should be to put in place the supports that will help him succeed where he is. If the school resists making such accommodations, you may have the law on your side (see page 115).

While I can't offer you legal advice, you should know that ADHD is considered a "disability" under the federal Americans with Disabilities Act. The act requires schools, camps, and other public facilities to make "reasonable" accommodations for such disabilities. In my view the accommodations a school must make for a child with ADHD—such as the ones described at the beginning of this chapter—are usually pretty reasonable.

What school wouldn't agree to let a child with poor eyesight sit near the blackboard? How many schools would refuse to give a student extra time to complete a test if she had a muscular disorder that slowed her handwriting? And why wouldn't they make similar accommodations for a child with ADHD?

If your school administrators and teachers aren't comfortable teaching children with ADHD, perhaps they need more information. If the resistance runs deeper than that, you'll have to decide what's best for your child. Perhaps it does make sense to find a more enlightened school. On the other hand, changing schools can be extremely disruptive and damaging to a child, especially if he believes he had to leave because he couldn't measure up to the school's standards.

I hope that as more people understand what ADHD is all about, these issues will come up far less frequently. ADHD is one of the most common childhood disorders. Every school, public and private, will encounter it and must address it.

What if the teacher doesn't "believe" in ADHD?

Parents of children with ADHD learn very early on that your child's teacher can make a world of difference—for better or for worse.

On one end of the spectrum is the teacher who simply doesn't accept the validity of the condition—or who accepts it only halfheartedly. One tends to think these would be older teachers, of the "spare the rod and spoil the child" school, but in fact we've seen it occur with teachers of all ages. In fact, more mature teachers, by virtue of many years of experience in the classroom, often know just what we're talking about when we describe the characteristics of ADHD in the classroom.

Teachers who don't "believe" in ADHD can do a lot of damage. If they view your child's behavior in moralistic terms—that your child is being "willful" or "disrespectful"—chances are good that no learning is taking place and your child's self-esteem is taking a nosedive.

If you encounter these kinds of attitudes—and thankfully they're becoming less common than in the past—you need to educate the educator. Bring in brochures and literature. A letter or phone call from your pediatrician can go a long way toward reinforcing the message. Make sure the administration is aware of how the teacher feels, and point out that such thinking runs counter to your own doctor's diagnosis and the great weight of medical evidence. Ask the school whether it has offered or plans to offer any training on ADHD for staff and teachers.

If none of these efforts has an impact, it's time for a heart-to-heart talk with the school nurse, principal, and guidance counselor. Though schools tend to be reluctant to switch children to different teachers, if you can demonstrate and document your concerns you may be able to convince them that neither the child's nor the teacher's interests are well served by the situation. At the very least, you can insist that the teacher implement appropriate classroom techniques for ADHD—such as the ones we discuss in this chapter.

And in this unfortunate situation, you'll need to work with your child as well. Explain what's happening in terms your child can understand: "Mrs. Miller thinks that when you speak out of turn you're just being rude, but we know that sometimes you can't help it." Help your child understand that there will be people throughout his life who will think this way, but that it doesn't mean they're right.

What kind of teacher is best for a child with ADHD?

Some teachers' personalities and teaching styles simply aren't good fits for an ADHD child.

Not surprisingly, we find that ADHD children do best with teachers who are flexible and who recognize and accommodate children's different learning styles. Teachers who ask questions, walk around the room during a lecture, and encourage hands-on exercises and a high degree of classroom participation will help a child with ADHD stay focused and engaged.

Also, some teachers focus more on the *how* of learning than the *what.* For example, they're more concerned with teaching children study techniques and organizational skills than simply imparting facts. These are the teachers who tell kids how to study for a spelling test rather than simply announcing that it will be next Tuesday. Clearly, the teacher who can teach the how-tos will be a boon to a child with ADHD.

Finally, there is the most important quality of all: patience. Teaching a child with ADHD can be frustrating, and some days it seems there's more ground lost than gained. A teacher who can take the long view, and consistently provide the right kind of learning environment, will do wonders for the child with ADHD.

Should I request a specific teacher for my child in the coming school year?

It depends a lot on the school.

Of course, you don't usually get to choose directly who your child's teacher will be. However, at the end of the school year, talk to your child's current teacher and the guidance counselor, and ask them to give some thought to which of the next grade's teachers will be the best fit for your child. And if you have a sense that a particular teacher would be an especially good or poor fit, find a diplomatic way to say so. (Remember, it's not a question of a teacher being "good" or "bad"; it's simply a question of how well his or her teaching style works with your child.) The school may not grant your request, but your insights should be taken into consideration when the school is making up assignments for next year.

Who should be responsible for administering medications in school?

This seemingly innocent question has touched off a lot of controversy recently, with some teachers, administrators, and even school nurses expressing reluctance to administer medications for ADHD.

In my view, there's no medical or scientific reason for concern, provided they're administering the medication in accordance with a doctor's prescription. Ritalin, Dexedrine, and other ADHD medications have an outstanding safety record in the treatment of ADHD. And occasional errors in administering the drugs aren't likely to cause any long-term harm.

The most common error is likely to be a missed dose. But since most of these drugs don't accumulate in the body, an occasional missed dose won't make a difference in the long run. If a child misses his midday dose, he'll probably have a difficult time in the afternoon, but once he takes his next scheduled dose he'll be back where he should be.

Potentially more serious is a case in which a child receives an incorrect dose—either because she inadvertently is given a second dose or because she gets someone else's prescription by accident. But here, too, the physical risks aren't that great if a child receives, say, a double dose on a single occasion. (Of course, it's still important to know that the mixup occurred, so that you don't think your child is having trouble tolerating her usual dosage. And if medication errors are occurring frequently, you need to find out why and ensure that the school promptly takes steps to fix the problem.)

Despite the relative safety of ADHD medications, however, a growing number of schools are refusing to get involved in administering them. Many cite the administrative burden; some also say they don't want to be responsible for making sure the child complies with his medication regimen.

We can debate whether these concerns are justified, but the bottom line is that if your school won't administer medication during school hours, you have a number of choices:

1. You can come to the school yourself every day to give your child his midday dose—which isn't a practical option for many parents.

2. You can make your child responsible for taking his own medication every day. This is a good choice for older children and younger ones who are motivated. But it may be an uphill battle for many children. Few of them like to take a pill in the first place, and the problem is compounded by the ADHD itself. If your child has trouble remembering to bring her

schoolbag at the end of the day, will she remember to take her medication at lunchtime?

3. You can help by giving the child reminders—for example, packing the medications right in her lunchbox. And even if the school has a policy against *administering* medications, you can certainly ask for its help in *reminding* your child to take them.

4. An alarm watch—some come with as many as five alarms—is a great way to remind the child to take his medication. Similarly, some pill cases have programmable alarms.

5. You can ask your doctor to consider a longer-acting stimulant such as Adderral, Dexedrine spansules, or sustained-release Ritalin, which may allow you to skip the midday dosage altogether.

Who monitors side effects?

Just as teachers and school counselors play an important role in identifying children at risk for ADHD, their observations will be important in helping you and the doctor evaluate any potential side effects. Ask the teacher to watch for signs that the child's medication needs to be adjusted for side effects, such as mood changes, irritability, and lack of appetite, or stomachaches, headaches, or other physical complaints.

How can I help my child's teacher?

Throughout this book, we've looked at many practical classroom strategies that you can share with your child's teacher. But there's one other thing you can do: Let the teacher know that she's doing a good job.

As we focus on the problems facing a child with ADHD, it's easy to overlook the *emotional* impact of this disorder on teachers. ADHD children are a challenge in the classroom, no matter how well informed, well intentioned, and skilled that teacher is—not just because the disorder is disruptive but because it challenges the teacher's own sense of competence.

Just as your child's ADHD can make you feel like a poor parent, it can make your child's teacher feel like a poor teacher. After all, what do good teachers pride themselves on? Their ability to engage the interest and enthusiasm of their students. Their ability to help a student absorb a lesson, whether it involves geography or rules of classroom participation. The ability to manage the classroom and create an environment that's conducive to learning.

ADHD challenges teachers on all these fronts. And even when teachers understand the *reasons* for ADHD, it's hard to set aside their emotional responses. Indeed, studies show that teachers with ADHD children in their classrooms tend to use more negative and disciplinary responses with *all* of the children in the class.

In an ideal world, teachers would always respond with kindness and empathy to a child with ADHD. In an ideal world, they would never lose their temper, get frustrated, or grow impatient.

So would parents, for that matter. But neither parents nor teachers are perfect. And while parents should never condone or acquiesce in harmful behavior or attitudes, it never hurts to show some empathy for the challenges the teacher faces. In fact, it will probably do wonders for your relationship—and your child's relationship—with a teacher.

So when you next have the opportunity, make a point of telling your child's teacher how much you appreciate her efforts on your child's behalf, and acknowledge that it must be frustrating at times. Teachers, like parents, need to hear that they're doing a good job under tough circumstances.

Are there some grades that are especially challenging for a child with ADHD?

In the early years, the first big adjustment comes in the first grade, when the child is first expected to sit quietly for long periods of time and to work independently. Another difficult transition comes in third grade because of the amount of reading that's involved. The transition from elementary to middle or junior high school is also challenging; not only is the child usually entering a new school, but he must change classes every period and juggle the sometimes conflicting requirements of several teachers. In addition, he will be expected to work more independently at this stage. And, of course, college is a big issue, for many reasons: The child is often away from home and from the supports parents provide for the first time; there's far less support within the school itself; and there are many more distractions.

What is the best classroom environment for a child with ADHD?

The ideal classroom will be *informal* but *structured*. That may sound contradictory at first, because we tend to think of structure and formality as being the same thing. They're not.

By "formal" I mean the type of classroom where all children are expected to sit in their seat and the teacher stands in front of the classroom delivering a lecture. Such an environment may *look* structured, but it isn't necessarily so. The lectures may be unfocused. The children may not be getting good guidelines on what's expected of them.

The problem with a formal classroom setting is that it presumes all children learn in the same way. Often an ADHD child needs more latitude in *how* (versus) *what* she accomplishes. For example, she may need to stand up at her desk and work at her own pace.

What are the characteristics of a structured classroom?

A well-*structured* classroom, on the other hand, can be highly informal. But it incorporates lots of cues and tools that help children organize their work and stay focused. For example, the teacher may post calendars, daily schedules, and assignments prominently, and refer to them often. Children will have a designated work space. Materials will be well organized—for example, art supplies will always be kept in the same closet; the dictionary will always be kept in the same spot on the teacher's desk. Short-term and long-term assignments will be written in the same corner of the blackboard.

The structure should extend into the child's personal area as well. For example, books and materials should be organized—and the organizational principles should be clear. ADHD children have notoriously messy desks. Sometimes they think that they're organizing when they're really just straightening—putting their books in a neat pile, putting their papers into folders. But if the math homework is still stuffed into the back of the folder and the math book is sitting on the bottom of the books because it happens to be the biggest, then the child hasn't really made any progress toward organization. Even if the end result isn't as neat, it's better to organize according to consistent principles. For example, the homework folder might be organized in the same order as the school day—if Johnny has math, reading, and geography in that order every day, his homework folder can have math first, then reading, then geography.

That brings up another point. *Time* should be well structured, too, day to day, week to week, and throughout the school year. Ideally, classes will follow the same schedule every day: Spelling always comes after math. English is always first, and so on. In many schools that degree of structure won't be practical, but the more consistent the schedule, the better for the ADHD child. The same goes for the week—for example, enrichment activities like art or music will always happen on Thursdays.

A bigger challenge is helping the child organize long periods of time—a semester, or a school year. ADHD children tend to have midseason slumps. At the beginning of the year their attention is held by the novelty of the new class. Toward April and May, the end is in sight and it helps them stay focused on what needs to get done. But the long stretch from midwinter to spring is a time when they're more likely to lose their way.

From the point of view of ADHD kids, a semester is a long, long time, and it's tough for them to maintain a consistent focus over the long haul. Just as with the classroom day or week, there should be a lot of organizational cues for the semester and school year. For example, a teacher may wish to post a set of goals and milestones at the beginning of the semester, and cross them off as each one is achieved. Similarly, one could post a time line for the semester above the blackboard, again highlighting special dates, objectives, and milestones. Once a week, the class can review the timeline and cross off what's been accomplished, and look ahead at what remains to be done.

These *external* cues help compensate for the ADHD child's *internal* organizational problems. Think of them as the painted stripes on a highway; they help keep the child from wandering all over the road. At the same time, they act as models that the child can use to develop his own organizational strategies. When we first learn to drive, we rely on those stripes a lot. Over time, we think about them less and less, but it still helps that they're there.

How should assignments be structured?

Because children with ADHD have trouble completing long sequences of tasks, a good technique for teachers and parents is to break them up into the smallest possible chunks. For example, it's preferable to give long homework assignments well in advance and permit the child do a little each day rather than all at once. If the child has a twenty-word spelling list, it will be easier to memorize four words a day over the week, rather than twenty all at once.

This "chunking" strategy also holds true for instructions in the classroom. At the end of the day, if the teacher tells the children to put away their books, put their homework assignments in their backpacks, get their coats, and line up for dismissal, the child with ADHD will still be looking for his backpack by the time the bell rings. But by breaking up these instructions into small chunks—and making sure each chunk is completed before moving on to the next one—the teacher can help the ADHD child stay focused. The teacher might say, "It's time to get ready to leave. Put your books away"—and then take a moment to ensure that everyone has done it. "Now put your homework assignments in your backpacks." And so on.

It may take awhile until this instructional style comes naturally. And over time, the teacher should look to raise the bar a little—to give two instructions instead of one. But this approach allows a child to succeed and acquire the organizational skills gradually, rather than being overwhelmed at the outset.

How should the teacher approach discipline?

First, teachers need to understand that often, ADHD children literally don't realize why they're in trouble. For example, when the teacher tells Susan not to interrupt and she says, "I didn't," it sounds like she's being argumentative or making excuses. In fact, Susan may have no idea she was interrupting. So from her point of view, she can't understand, first, why she was accused of something she didn't do, and second, why the teacher won't let her defend herself.

In one study, a group of non-ADHD children and those with ADHD were given fictional scenarios of disruptive behavior and asked to explain what was going on. A significant difference emerged: Most children thought that the child in the example *could* have controlled his behavior if he chose to; those with ADHD thought the fictional child *couldn't* control the behavior, and they identified outside forces that provoked it—for example, "His friends bug him all the time."

From the perspective of someone with ADHD, this view makes perfect sense. They know that in many cases they themselves *can't* control their own behavior. So it's not surprising that they feel persecuted when a teacher, parent, or peer blames them for their actions. If you got blamed because it happened to rain on your picnic, you'd feel persecuted too.

In the classroom, the teacher must walk the fine line between responsibility and blame. It's important for the teacher to impart a sense of responsibility to the child for his actions, and to help him understand the consequences of those acts—but to do it in a way that doesn't make the child feel persecuted.

It's a tough challenge. One way to approach it is by acknowledging the difficulties while expressing confidence in the child's ability to overcome them and offering a concrete strategy for doing so. For example, the teacher might tell a child, "I know it's hard for you to sit still on the bus. I think it will be easier if you sit next to me so that I can remind you to sit down." Even though the outcome may be the same, that approach sends a much more positive message than simply telling the child to sit next to you on the bus.

My child's teacher always tells him when he's doing something wrong. But my child never hears what he's doing right. Isn't there a better way to deal with ADHD?

Yes, there is. Positive reinforcement is one of the most powerful techniques in the classroom—for all students, not just those with ADHD. Over the long term, it's the best way to shape behavior. It has beneficial effects not only on the child who's receiving the praise, but on the teacher who's giving the praise and the other students, too.

But it's also one of the most underused tools. All of us, teachers included, tend to use criticism rather than praise when we're trying to shape behavior. One study found that teachers offer more praise than criticism only through the second grade. And most of the praise that *is* given is for academics—for example, praising a child for giving the right answer. The amount of positive reinforcement for classroom *behavior* (arguably the area where it will do the most good) is close to zero.

I don't think that happens because teachers are especially mean or critical people. It's just the nature of the classroom environment. If the classroom is humming along and everything is going well, the teacher isn't likely to be thinking about behavioral issues. Like the students, he or she will probably be engaged in the lesson.

It's only when this process gets disrupted that the teacher's attention is focused on the behavioral issue. And the teacher's impulse will likely be to fix the behavioral problem quickly and get back to the "real work." Criticism or punishment offers such a quick fix. Positive reinforcement is more effective in the long run, but the payoff usually isn't as immediate.

Also, we don't need to be *reminded* to offer criticism. Inappropriate behavior triggers it automatically. But we all tend to take appropriate behavior for granted. We don't thank fellow drivers for stopping at red lights—but we sure let them know when they run one. We don't call the personnel office when our paychecks arrive on time—only when they don't. When we go to school conferences, we spend precious little time reviewing the subjects where the child is making A's and B's. We focus on the problem areas.

It's not surprising that the same thing happens in the classroom. Virtually every teacher knows how important positive reinforcement is, but in the rush of the school day few give it the attention it deserves.

Teachers can change their own behavior using the same techniques they employ with students. For example, one of the simplest ways is to keep a tally of how frequently they offer praise versus criticism. The tally—kept, perhaps, on an inconspicuous corner of the teacher's desk—can be a daily reminder to use praise to reinforce desirable behavior.

The results of such simple interventions can be dramatic. For example, one report showed that a child's time on task increased from 62 percent to 96 percent when a teacher switched from criticism to praise.

What other behavioral approaches can my child's teacher use?

The National Institutes of Mental Health offers three behavioral strategies for ADHD that can be used in ordinary classrooms. Though they're substantially more involved than the other approaches I've described, they've all been used in actual classroom settings to good effect.

The first is known as a currency-based token economy. It uses tokens to reward children for appropriate behavior, and imposes "fines" for inappropriate behavior. The program uses play money, and the rewards and fines are fairly substantial so that the child can earn "dollars" quickly. For example, staying seated earns a child $10 in tokens; chair tipping results in a $5 fine. The teacher dispenses rewards and fines according to her expectations for each individual child; one child may earn a reward after five minutes in his seat, another after twenty minutes. And as behavior improves, the teacher can raise the expectations accordingly.

Children save their tokens in "bank pouches," and they're permitted to cash them in once a week (or daily for younger children). The children are allowed to choose from a variety of privileges—for example, playing a game, borrowing a book to take home, computer time, or being the classroom messenger for a week.

The second model uses "happy faces" instead of play money, and the teacher gives a great deal of paise when she distributes them. Like the tokens, the happy faces can be redeemed for privileges.

A third approach uses contracts, mutually agreed upon by the teacher and the individual child, addressing a specific problem, the strategies the child will employ to solve it, the assistance she will need, and the reinforcement or reward that she will earn upon completing it. The contract emphasizes positive and specific goals, for example: "to stay in my seat" rather than "to stop jumping out of my seat." Generally, the contracts are short-term, with the reward coming no more than a week after the contract is initiated.

These suggestions sound great, but I know that if I suggested them to my child's teacher she'd think I was trying to tell her how to do her job.

Like the rest of us, most teachers have a considerable emotional investment in their jobs, and consciously or unconsciously they may resent "outsiders"—especially parents—telling them how to do it better. It's part of human nature, but it's unfortunate, because teachers could learn a lot from parents of children with special needs. Of necessity, these parents have usually become experts in the issues affecting their children.

In many cases, ideas such as the ones we've looked at here are more readily accepted if they're offered in a broader context, as training for a group of teachers. For example, you may wish to work through a group like C.h.A.D.D. (see chapter 10) to conduct a seminar for teachers on managing ADHD in the classroom. In this context, it's not you against the teacher; it's an organization offering training that can help teachers enhance their professional skills.

How can the school help my child with peer issues?

ADHD children often need extra help in forming healthy peer relationships. One way the teacher and school can help is by incorporating into the curriculum structured activities that involve the child with his or her peers in noncompetitive activities—for example, classroom skits, group projects, and so on.

Also, because ADHD kids are often outsiders, the teacher can look for opportunities to raise your child's status in the classroom—for example, by assigning him to be hall monitor, line leader, and so on. Clearly, these privileges must be handled carefully. If the child and his peers think he's consistently being singled out for special attention, the strategy could backfire and simply make other children feel resentful.

But there are other, day-to-day ways a teacher can give out cues—asking the child to hand out materials, starting a class discussion by putting a question to the child, and so on. In group projects, the teacher can pair the child with popular partners. Some of the partners' popularity will reflect back on the child.

Another strategy is to enlist the help of another child in the class who is empathic and well regarded. For example, a teacher might take another child aside and say something like, "I have a favor to ask of you. Have you noticed that Jennifer has trouble making friends? I think she must be very lonely. Since the other kids in the class look up to you so much, I thought that together you and I could find ways to help her be more a part of the group. Can you think of any things we might be able to do?"

What are some strategies that will help my child with his homework?

Homework really begins in the classroom, and it's important for the child to have a *simple, consistent,* and *compelling* system for taking down the assignment and bringing it home. A homework folder or assignment book is a must. The teacher can help by explicitly reminding the class at the end of the day to put the assignment into their backpacks.

In addition to the assignment, your child will also need the necessary materials to complete it—worksheets, word lists, textbooks, and the like. Most of the materials can be kept in the folder, but books are a bigger problem. If, despite everyone's best efforts, your child still can't seem to remember his books, consider getting a second set to keep at home. Some might argue that this undermines the child's responsibility to bring books home, but as a parent you have to weigh this benefit against the drawback of the child's not being able to complete the assignment at all.

Similarly, it's a good idea to enlist a "homework buddy" whom you can call for the assignment if the child forgets. Here, too, some might question whether a child will be less motivated to remember the assignment if he knows he can call someone and get it over the phone. But there's more to homework than simply bringing home the assignment. And all in all, it's better that a child have an opportunity to complete the assignment and turn it in, rather than be subjected to the anxiety and humiliation of not having his homework the next day in class.

Homework should be done at the same time and same place every day. And as with schoolwork, the more structures and routines, the better—for example, doing the assignments for each class in the same order every day.

What sort of environment is best for homework?

Traditionally, it's been recommended that a child with ADHD have a quiet, separate space for homework. That's generally true, but you have to be careful that it's not *too* quiet or *too* separate. If you send Billy up to his neat, quiet desk in a room free from distractions, you might look in on him an hour later and find out he hasn't even started. It's tough to strike a balance, but the ideal area will be quiet and distraction free, while still in an area where you can supervise what's going on.

A number of parents have reported success with a "family" approach to homework, where, for example, the children work at the kitchen table while Mom sits across from them and pays the bills. This approach allows the parent to keep the child on task while still establishing a degree of independence.

There's no one right answer to this question. Some kids need total silence. Some need to have white noise in the background to drown out distractions. Some work best alone, others when they're in the middle of things. Experiment and find out what works best for you and your child.

Should I hire a tutor to help my child with her homework?

It depends on a number of factors. ADHD children learn well in one-on-one settings, so having someone to help with homework can be a lifesaver. Often that's a parent, but the problem is that the parent isn't just "someone," so there are a lot of emotional issues for both participants.

If you find yourself constantly locking horns with your child over homework issues, a tutor or homework companion can be a godsend. ADHD parents and children must face many other issues, so if a tutor can take this one off the table, it can vastly improve the parent-child relationship. And because a tutor can approach the situation with more detachment than the parent, the experience is often less stressful and more productive from the child's point of view as well.

One caveat: This kind of assistance is often useful in helping a child with ADHD make up for lost ground and fill in gaps in their learning. But when ADHD is complicated by learning disabilities, the child needs a learning specialist, not a tutor. In fact, a tutor can be detrimental (see pages 85–86).

Is the school required to make accommodations for my child's ADHD?

Under the law, public schools are required to make "reasonable" accommodations for ADHD children. In September 1991, the Department of Education issued guidelines clarifying that ADHD is an "other health impaired disability" and that accommodations for ADHD are a right under Civil Rights Code, Section 504, and Public Law 94-142. Thus, both regular education and special education students must be provided support as needed for problems caused by their ADHD.

Obviously, there's a lot of room for interpretation in these guidelines, but keep in mind that the accommodations required for an ADHD child—for example, moving his desk to the front of the class or making provisions for untimed tests—are usually low-cost or no-cost and easily implemented.

The law doesn't set out what, specifically, constitutes a reasonable accommodation, recognizing that it will be different for each child and each school. Most schools, law or no law, will take the steps that are necessary to help a student succeed. But when you run up against an official attitude of "That's not how we do things here," the Americans with Disabilities Act gives you ammunition to help make some changes.

In one area, standardized tests, the Act has made a significant difference. Because of the effects of ADHD on attention and motor skills, these children tend to do poorly on timed tests, even if they know the material. But if your child has been diagnosed with ADHD, test rules often permit the child to take an untimed test.

But isn't this cheating?

No—not any more than allowing a child with vision problems to have someone read the questions and answers to her out loud. There are two basic kinds of standardized tests—achievement and aptitude. The first measures *what* you've learned so far. The second measures your *ability* to learn new things. Neither type is intended to measure how quickly you can fill in little dots on a sheet.

What is an IEP?

An Individualized Education Plan—required by law for public schools—sets forth a specific plan to remove or minimize barriers to a child's learning. The law requires schools to develop such a plan for children with disabilities—a sort of road map that describes how educational and social issues will be addressed and the strategies that the school will put into place. The plan is developed by a "child study team," consisting of the teacher, learning specialist, counselor, school psychologist, or other professionals.

While it all sounds good in theory, there's a lot of variation in the quality of such plans. Some are excellent, but in some schools you tend to get an off-the-shelf solution that may or may not be right for your child. And in the real world, there are often unspoken economic issues at play, where schools tend to favor lower-cost strategies. For example, it costs nothing to put a child in the front of the classroom, but a learning specialist or tutor can be expensive.

Therefore, you have a key role to play in the development of the school's IEP. It's often up to the parents to act as advocates, and to be sure their child is getting what she needs and is entitled to under the law. And there's certainly a role for your doctor to play as well—rightly or wrongly, schools often give more weight to a phone call from a doctor than from a parent. Or you may have to bring in other professionals—for example, hire an independent learning specialist to review the IEP and prod the school to improve it if necessary. Sometimes you may even need the help of a lawyer.

I'm not suggesting that such drastic steps are always, or even usually, necessary. And certainly it's better for everyone, including your child, if your relationship with the school is one of cooperation, not confrontation. But keep in mind that the school may be distracted by other issues besides what's best for your child. It's your job, as parent and advocate, to help them stay focused and put your child's needs first.

Are private schools bound by these same requirements?

Most private schools aren't covered by these accommodation requirements. Most will make reasonable accommodations as a matter of policy, but they're not required to under the law. And in some cases, they may provide additional help, such as learning specialists, but charge extra for these services.

However, many private schools follow the spirit of these laws voluntarily. For example, they may use child study teams and proactively seek out strategies to help ADHD students achieve their full potential.

A school that resists making these kinds of changes usually does so out of ignorance, because most are neither costly nor difficult to implement. In fact, you may be able to convince the school that these accommodations help not only the few children who have ADHD but also the school as a whole. For example, they help minimize classroom disruptions caused by ADHD children and the amount of time the teacher must spend on discipline. What's more, they can help teachers develop new teaching strategies that will be useful with all children, not just ADHD children (for example, by increasing the amount of positive reinforcement that the teacher gives). And, finally, a classroom that can accommodate different learning styles can teach a lot about tolerance and the positive values of diversity.

Can I—and should I—keep the diagnosis from appearing in my child's permanent school record?

You might be able to, but you'll do your child a disservice by trying to hide his condition. So far as I know, no high school or college has a policy to exclude an applicant because he or she has ADHD. In fact, such a policy would be illegal. On the contrary, if the school knows about your child's condition, it can put the kinds of support in place that will promote success.

But this question does raise the issue of labeling. By telling the teacher and administration that your child has ADHD, you will affect their perceptions of him. If a "normal" child loses his pencil or has a messy desk, the teacher probably wouldn't give it too much thought. But with an ADHD child, the teacher may see it as "disruptive" or evidence that the child isn't adapting well to the classroom environment.

How can you head off this possibility? The solution isn't to get rid of the label but to help teachers and schools get *past* it. Sure, your child has ADHD. Yes, there are strategies that should be in place to address those issues in the classroom. But after you and the school have adopted those strategies, it's time to move on with the task of educating your child.

One place you may encounter this labeling tendency is at teacher-parent conferences. You may find, for example, that the teacher's report focuses almost exclusively on your child's ADHD and the problems it causes. If so, use the conference as an opportunity to refocus the teacher's thinking toward your child's *potential* instead of her *limitations*. You might, for example, take a matter-of-fact view toward ADHD: "Yes, Miss Jones, I appreciate the steps you and the school are taking to address Janey's attentional problems. I'm satisfied we're all doing the best we can in that area. But tell me, apart from those issues, how Janey is doing."

And, of course, it's perfectly acceptable to raise the issue head-on: "You know, I'm concerned that as Janey goes through school, people will tend to focus on the ADHD label so much that they won't see her as a whole person. I don't want her to start thinking of herself as 'an ADHD kid.' I want her to think of herself as a regular kid who happens to have ADHD. So I wonder: What can we do this year to make sure she doesn't get stuck with that label?"

The school recommends that we hold my daughter back a grade so that she'll have a chance to mature. Is this a good idea?

It's hard to say without knowing all the details, but as a general rule there's no benefit in keeping a child with ADHD back a grade in the hope that she'll "mature."

Studies of men with ADHD have shown that their behavior remained socially immature into mid-adult life. This would argue against retaining a child in a grade because of social immaturity. It would be much better to provide an environment where the opportunity for success is enhanced, so that self-esteem is preserved.

My child tells me that his teacher singles him out for ridicule and picks on him. Of course, the teacher denies it. Who's lying?

It's quite possible that neither the teacher nor the child is lying. They're just seeing the same events from different perspectives.

Because ADHD children feel that they can't control their behavior, they often come to believe—quite sincerely—that the teacher is blaming them for things that aren't their fault. And their difficulty in attending to social cues reinforces this sense. They often don't realize how their own acts contribute to the difficulties they face. The upshot is that they may feel persecuted.

In this situation, try to help your child acquire some insight into the consequences of his or her behavior—without blaming. For example, you might pose a series of questions to your child: "What is Mr. Lewis's number one job? That's right, teaching. Now, if you were a teacher and a student was talking while you were teaching, wouldn't that make it harder to do your job? And to do your number one job, wouldn't you have to ask that child to stop?"

Of course, that's not to say that every teacher is a paragon of patience, either. As you know, dealing with ADHD behavior can be extremely frustrating, and we have to recognize that teachers face those frustrations too. And in such circumstances, it's possible that the teacher lacks some objectivity about his own behavior, too.

Ultimately, this sort of student-teacher conflict isn't about one being right and the other wrong. It can only be resolved if both sides win. Often it's enough to meet one-on-one with the teacher and simply tell him what the child feels, along with some insights into why ADHD children often feel this way. Then go home and do the same with your child—tell him how the teacher feels. I've seen many cases where a parent conveying these feelings between the child and teacher, without accusations or blame to either party, has helped forge an especially warm and close relationship between a teacher and a child.

My child is doing okay in school, but I have the feeling she could be doing better. The teachers say she's working at her level and everything's fine. I know not everyone can be an A student, but am I right to be worried?

You've described one of the toughest dilemmas a parent can face. In this situation, you run the risk of looking like a parent who's simply overinvested in their child's grades, and it may be tough to get people to take your concerns seriously.

As I mentioned earlier, not everyone is an A student, and there's nothing wrong with that. But a child can be doing "okay" by outside standards and still not be following their personal track to fulfillment.

In my experience, I find that parents' gut feelings are often a pretty good indicator of a problem. So if everyone is telling you that your child is doing fine but you still have a nagging feeling, listen to it.

ADHD and other conditions such as dyslexia or anxiety can't be diagnosed with a report card. If there's a problem, it can be detected with the evaluation methods we describe in the next chapter. This is a case in which your role as advocate becomes paramount: Far too many cases of ADHD are overlooked because the child is not in crisis. It's much much better to make the diagnosis at that point, so that we can prevent the consequences of this disorder rather than having to undo them later on!

CHAPTER 8

Home, Family, and Friends

The ability to initiate and maintain relationships with other people is fundamental to one's sense of self and well-being. ADHD, by interfering with the ability to pick up and respond to social cues, can cause social problems throughout life. Treatment and the support strategies outlined in this chapter can prevent these problems.

Why is it hard for my child to make friends?

The social consequences of ADHD get a lot less attention than issues like school and work performance. That's unfortunate, because the disorder can cause as many problems with interpersonal relationships as with schoolwork. In fact, these problems are potentially more far-reaching. I know many happy and well-adjusted people who never did well in school. But I've yet to have anyone tell me that good grades can take the place of good friends.

This issue gets short shrift, I suspect, because it's hard to measure social success. If your child flunks a test or doesn't finish her homework, you'll know there's a problem right away. But you don't get a report card on social interactions.

Also, people tend to view social skills like eye color or height: a fundamental and unchangeable attribute. "She's shy," we'll say, or "He's not outgoing." When you think about how you make a friend, it seems almost magical; it just happens, right?

Well, if you look at it closely, it *doesn't* just happen. Instinctively, we engage in certain rituals. For example, the first step usually involves cautious probing to find common ground: a mutual acquaintance, a shared experience.

We're not born with such skills; they must be learned, just like academic skills. Sure, some people have more aptitude for making friends, just like some people are good with numbers. But when our child doesn't know his multiplication tables, we don't just throw up our hands and assume it's destiny. If he has trouble with math, it simply means he has to work harder at it.

Social skills are harder to learn. We tend to acquire them unconsciously, rather than by formal instruction. Also, these are subtle skills. It's often hard to pin down the deficiencies exactly; instead, people simply feel uncomfortable or irritable when dealing with a person whose skills are lacking, without knowing exactly why.

Does medication help with these problems?

If a child doesn't know how to read a sentence, the problem is easily identified. It may not be easy to fix, but at least everybody knows what to work on. But if a child doesn't know how to "read" the moods of a classmate, it can be extremely difficult for the parents, the teacher, the classmate, and the child himself to know where the problem lies. All we see is that Timmy doesn't like Billy, and would rather play with Stephanie.

But it seems that the two kinds of "reading" aren't as different as they seem. Both require careful and sustained attention. And so we see that ADHD treatments have effects on social performance mirroring those seen for academic performance.

The most dramatic improvements involve negative behaviors, such as noncooperation and disruption. Children taking medication for ADHD are better able to work and play independently; they listen to their parents better, and they're less domineering with their peers.

Unfortunately, but not surprisingly, research also shows that perception lags behind reality, especially among other children. For example, if you begin treatment of a child with ADHD and put him or her among a group of children who don't know one another, these children won't be able to see much difference between the ADHD child and non-ADHD children. But the children within his or her own peer group will continue to judge him or her according to past experience. Even when teachers and others report changes in the child's behavior, the other children won't see much of a change.

While that's a natural response, it's one that's bound to create problems for your ADHD child. It means that even after treatment begins, your child will probably continue to have social difficulties. A radical solution is the "clean slate" approach—to put the child in a different school or class, to switch camps. A less radical approach is to counsel your child that acceptance may take some time, and to work with the school to promote new opportunities for peer interaction. For example, the teacher may be able to assign a new partner for a class project or find other ways to bring together children who don't know one another well. Finally, keep in mind that the problems of being "outside the in-group" aren't limited to children with ADHD; you might suggest that the school work with the class as a whole on such issues.

Also, consider taking an active role in promoting social activities and ensuring that interactions are successful and enjoyable. These activities give you a chance to help coach your child in social skills in a controlled environment. At the same time, successful interactions will help change other children's perceptions of your child. And those perceptions, shared through the playground grapevine, will extend beyond the group that is actually there.

Another way in which medication enhances the social relationships of children with ADHD is the effect it has on their own feelings—and whether they react to a situation with anger or acceptance. In one study, children taking Ritalin and those taking placebos were asked to react to statements such as "being blamed for something that was not your fault" and "your friends making fun of you." Children on medications were less likely to react to such statements with aggression or hostility; they were able to take them in stride.

Besides medication, what else can I do to help my child acquire these skills?

First, it's an enormous help just knowing that the problem is usually a skill deficit, not an aspect of personality. That gives you and your child a lot of hope: Though we can't change personality, we can definitely upgrade skills.

But before you let your child in on this secret, first find opportunities to observe unobtrusively how your child interacts with others—family members, peers, and people he's just met. Also, look at how these other people react to him. What specific behaviors does your child use that seem to go wrong? Does he talk more than listen? Ask questions that are inappropriate? Fail to make eye contact?

And what cues is he not picking up from the other person? A rising inflection, perhaps, or an attempt to change the subject. Look at how, and when, the other person withdraws.

With careful observation, there's a good chance you'll find certain patterns occurring over and over again. For example, the impulsivity of ADHD, which makes these children prone to call out in the classroom, often makes them more prone to ask inappropriate, personal, or embarrassing questions of someone they've just met. And their problems with attention often make them appear to be uninterested in what others have to say.

After you've made these observations, you can sit down with your child and talk about how ADHD affects her ability to make and keep friends. Look for what educators call a "teachable moment"—a time when your child is grappling with these problems herself.

Using your previous observations as a guide, you and your child can probably agree on three or four key skills to work on first. By presenting it this way, you gain three big advantages: (1) You make the problem manageable for you and your child. Now you don't have to worry about micromanaging every social encounter. Even if you see other social problems come up from time to time, you can let them pass and focus your energies on the most important ones. (2) It establishes an atmosphere of learning and cooperation. You can be a teacher to your child instead of nagging her about manners or trying to force friendships. (3) It removes the element of shame and replaces it with a positive outlook. It can be a tremendous boost to a child's self-esteem to view social deficiencies as skills not yet learned rather than character flaws.

My child says the kids at school think she's a geek. How can I get them to like her?

There's no way *you* can get other kids to like yours. Only your child can do that. In fact, any attempts by parents usually backfire. Either the other child resents the pressure or views your child as an object of pity. It's better to put effort toward teaching your child social skills, and helping her practice them.

As I mentioned in Chapter 7, sometimes the help of another child can be enlisted to introduce your child to a peer group. But that's not the same as trying to recruit a friend for your child. It's more of an icebreaker, just as you might help two of your friends get to know one another.

It's always difficult for parents to see their child struggling and not want to intervene. But that's how learning happens. Just as you wouldn't take your child's spelling test for him, so you can't broker his social life.

However, you can *facilitate* it by finding opportunities for your child to make friends. With families' hectic schedules these days, it seems there's not much time between the child's school and homework and parents' jobs. But if your child is finding it difficult to connect at school, other peer groups can be a godsend—especially if those groups are ones that play to your child's strengths and interests. For example, many children with ADHD love to act. An acting workshop might provide a peer group that celebrates and rewards your child's talents, without the baggage that comes from difficulties in the classroom or the schoolyard.

What else can I do to help my child make friends?

One thing is to accept the fact that your child may end up with friends that you wouldn't have picked. I'm not talking about letting your kid fall in with a bad crowd—in fact, you have to be extra vigilant to make sure that the peer group is one that promotes positive values. But sometimes parents and children alike fall into the trap of looking for friends whose stellar qualities will somehow rub off on those they associate with.

In reality, the best friend for your child may not be the quiet, straight-A student. If you think about it, people usually become friends because of shared experiences and values. We like our friends because they know where we're coming from.

So don't be surprised, for example, if your child's best friend ends up being another child with ADHD. It may be the best thing that ever happened to her. (Alcoholics Anonymous, for example, teaches that only alcoholics can truly help other alcoholics recover. And they're right: The best insights often come from someone who's already been there.)

On the other hand, your child may end up being best friends with the valedictorian. The point is, you never know what's going to make a friendship work.

One big problem area for us is sports. My son always gets picked last for teams.

Sports can be a devastating experience for kids with ADHD. One researcher looked at the differences in how ADHD children played baseball when they were taking Ritalin versus when they weren't.

It turns out that Ritalin has no effect on ADHD children's athletic skills per se. And yet, in the eyes of their peers, they still did better.

Why? It seems that on the sandlot, effort counts for a lot more than skill. Kids will tend to make allowances for someone who doesn't hit well or isn't quick enough around the bases. They're much less forgiving of the child who doesn't seem to care about the game—the child who's picking flowers when the fly ball comes in, or the one who manages to field the ball but then has no idea where to throw it. Presumably, kids feel that the child who engages in such behavior is letting the team down, and believe that such behavior, as opposed to athletic talent or skills, is within the child's control.

Which sports are best?

ADHD children do better at some sports than others, and they do better in some positions than others. Right field—which is where the kid who gets picked last tends to end up—is probably the worst possible position for a child with ADHD. Not much happens, you're far away from the action, and you're all by yourself. When these children play catcher or pitcher, on the other hand, the pace of the game is much different and helps keep them focused on the task.

Also, ADHD children generally do better at sports that involve a lot of movement and a lot of physical feedback. Skiing and hockey, for example, are good sports for someone with ADHD: The constantly shifting positions of the body, feet, and equipment keep the attention focused. One caution, though: Even with these sports, practice sessions are often difficult for ADHD kids, because of the slow and repetitive pace.

What is the impact of ADHD on the rest of the family?

When there's one family member with ADHD, we often see a particular family dynamic. Here's how it goes:

Early on—long before there's any diagnosis—moms seem instinctively to sense something's wrong. If she has other children, she may see a difference in development. But even with first children, there's often a subtle sense that the child is struggling.

I'm struck by how it's almost always the mother who picks up on this first. Of course, moms are still usually the ones who spend the most time as primary caregivers, so that's one reason. I think there is also a basic maternal instinct about these things as well. Consciously or unconsciously, the mother's response is to protect the child by making accommodations.

Fathers take a different path. Generally, they don't believe there's anything wrong with the child. Then, as the evidence mounts—poor school performance, behavior problems, social isolation—they usually conclude that it's all the mother's fault. She "coddles" the child; the child is "spoiled." That's what's causing the problems.

As time goes on, these two views become locked in a kind of emotional cold war: The father seeks to discipline the child, and views the mother as undermining his authority. The mother, in turn, sees herself as the protector, shielding the child from what she sees as the father's anger and harshness. Between the parents, there's blame, recrimination, and conflict; meanwhile, they're paralyzed because they can't agree on a consistent response to the child.

The child, of course, now has to carry not only his own burden of shame at not succeeding, but also a sense that he's breaking up his parents' marriage. Typically, the dynamic becomes the mother and child against the father.

What happens to the siblings?

As you might imagine, if there are siblings, they end up on the sidelines. As the family dynamic becomes centered around the ADHD child, the other kids feel (usually justifiably) like they're left out. And you see that feeling expressed in a variety of behaviors: They may withdraw. They may get into trouble as a way of attracting attention. They may drive themselves to make straight A's, feeling it's their responsibility to make up for the other child's deficiencies.

And typically, there's a lot of resentment directed at the ADHD sibling. Like the kids on the playground, there's little forgiveness for the child who seems like he's just not trying to make things better. I once had a patient whose brother had ADHD. She told me she'd resented him for a long time. "He stole my childhood," she said. "When I was growing up, everything was about him."

How can a family ever get over that kind of damage? Even after the child is treated, can it ever get past all that bad history?

One of the most remarkable things I see in my practice is how quickly families *do* recover once the child is diagnosed and treated. It's miraculous how resilient most families turn out to be. With diagnosis and treatment, all of these seemingly intractable problems start to melt away, and soon—often within just a few months—these families start to feel like normal happy families again.

I hear from time to time about how mothers are "invested" in their child's disorder, and how they'll undermine efforts at treatment because they can't give up the role of protector. But I've rarely seen it happen in my practice. Moms are only too glad to transfer that job to a professional. Once we find that there *is* in fact a problem and there *is* help for that problem, their burden is lifted.

Likewise with fathers. As the behavioral problems diminish, so does the need to blame the mother or up the ante on discipline. The parents suddenly find themselves with the time and emotional energy to reach out to each other and to the siblings. I've seen little evidence of *anyone*—parents, child, siblings, teacher—who stays "invested" in this disorder any longer than they have to.

Will the family need therapy to sort everything out after treatment begins? Usually, yes. Will there be residual damage from all the pain the family suffered in the past? Absolutely. But the good news is that most families do recover, and more quickly than you might expect.

What rules and strategies should exist in the home?

Many of the strategies we looked at in the chapter on schools apply to the home as well. Basically, a child with ADHD needs structure and routines: regular meals; a well-ordered environment—for example, labeled shelves and cubbyholes to organize toys; set routines—for example, doing homework in the same place and time every day; a regular bedtime.

And speaking of bedtime, I can't overemphasize how important a good night's sleep is for a child with ADHD. If you think about it, most of the key symptoms of ADHD—inattention, impulsivity, even hyperactivity—are all associated with fatigue, too. That "wired" feeling you get when you're running on too little sleep isn't all that different from what occurs in ADHD. The severity of symptoms will be directly related to how much rest your child gets.

How can I tell if my ADHD child or adolescent is in trouble?

In Chapter 6, we examined some of the warning signs for conduct disorder, depression, and other problems that often accompany ADHD. These signs can alert you to problems.

In a broader sense, any significant change in behavior should raise a red flag. It may be nothing. It may simply be normal developmental changes. But because of the risks associated with ADHD, you need to be extra vigilant. If you're not sure whether there's a problem or not, consult your doctor.

Does the family need counseling?

Probably, for a while. But the good news is that in most cases, family dynamics quickly change for the better once the ADHD is treated.

In my practice, I've seen classic cases of "dysfunctional families" centered around the problems of an ADHD child, with problems so severe and long-standing that you wonder how they'll ever get sorted out: the mother in the role of protector; the father in the role of enforcer; the child learning to manipulate the emotions of one parent against the other; the siblings ignored and resentful. These families look like candidates for years of therapy and heartache.

And yet often, as we treat the child for ADHD, we find that the family turns out to be remarkably resilient. Freed from the feelings of guilt and blame, as well as the stresses of the ADHD itself, these families often repair themselves with little if any professional help. The mother quickly relinquishes her "protector" role once the child is able to manage his own life more effectively; parents reestablish healthy bonds with their other children and with one another. A year or so later, you'd never know that this had ever been anything other than a stable, normal family.

This kind of happy ending is especially likely if treatment begins early. As time goes on, the psychological and family issues surrounding ADHD become more entrenched, and often require a lot of counseling.

CHAPTER 9

Looking Ahead

Doctors used to believe that children eventually outgrew ADHD. Today we recognize that the disorder doesn't disappear at adolescence; it changes. The hyperactivity tends to be redirected inward, transformed into a kind of internal restlessness. And the other key symptoms—inattention and impulsivity—continue into adulthood as well.

Among adults, untreated ADHD gives rise to a host of problems. For example, it may make it difficult to hold a steady job or work within a typical corporate structure. It may cause relationship problems. It may make it hard to get a college degree. It may lead to drug or alcohol dependency.

For all these reasons, virtually all experts agree today that ADHD needs to be treated over the person's entire lifetime. Discontinuing treatment at adolescence puts the obstacles of ADHD back in place at a critical time in one's development—arguably, a time when the child can least afford them.

Are there special risks related to adolescence and ADHD?

Adolescence is often a watershed for people with ADHD. Without proper treatment and support, an adolescent with

ADHD is at grave risk for depression, feelings of low self-esteem, and a sense of failure.

Adolescents usually develop ways to cope with the negative social consequences of ADHD, but without positive guidance they may "cope" by withdrawing, hanging out with a "bad crowd" (where their school and social problems are tolerated or even celebrated). They may seek to self-medicate or at least blunt negative feelings with drugs or alcohol. They may seek out stimulation through dangerous and high-risk activities, such as speeding or petty crime. They are also prone to be more sexually active, with multiple partners.

If left unchecked, these kinds of activities tend to become a self-fulfilling prophecy. For example, the more the adolescent withdraws from school and seeks approval from his peer group, the more isolated he becomes from teachers, parents, and other students.

Fortunately, most of these problems can be headed off with early treatment. And even for people who are misdiagnosed in childhood, treatment that begins later in life often has a dramatic effect on these problems. In fact, an accurate diagnosis, in and of itself, can have a profound and positive effect: It removes much of the self-blame and shame to know that these difficulties have a biochemical basis, and don't happen because one is "lazy" or "stupid."

How is adult ADHD different from childhood ADHD?

The underlying disorder isn't all that different, except for the fact that the hyperactivity tends to be more inwardly directed (that is, it manifests as a sense of inner restlessness rather than physical activity). But the *consequences* of the disorder may be very different. In general, as one gets older there are fewer supports in place to help, and a greater degree of independence.

On the one hand, that creates more difficulties for someone with ADHD—without others to provide guidance and structure, life can be more difficult. But at the same time, the transition to adulthood gives people greater flexibility. As an adult, you have more choices—about the kinds of work you do, about the way you live, about the methods that you choose to get things done. When you're making career choices, for example, you have a lot more options to choose from, and you don't have to lock yourself into a desk job. For many with ADHD, this flexibility can help them structure their lives in ways that take advantage of their strengths.

How is treatment different for adults?

It isn't. The same medications and techniques that are effective for childhood ADHD are also effective in adults. Of course, an adult's environment is different from a child's—the workplace isn't quite like the classroom. But even so, many of the organizational techniques of the classroom translate well into home and work for adults: the use of organizers to keep work on track, reminder systems, breaking up longer tasks into manageable chunks, and so forth.

The social issues facing children and adults with ADHD are similar, though they may emerge in different ways. For example, peer issues in childhood—making and keeping friends, fitting into the group and so on—often become the intimacy issues of adulthood. We use many of the same techniques for both groups.

Are there any specific risks or side effects from ADHD medications for adults that relate to fertility or sexuality?

None that we know of. ADHD medications have no known effects on fertility or sexuality. ADHD medications have proven to be safe for adults, as for children.

Is treatment that begins in adulthood as effective as treatment that begins in childhood?

Medically, the answer is yes—the medications work the same in adults as in children. However, by adulthood people have made many accommodations to the disorder. Some are helpful, but others—such as career choices—may be limiting. So the earlier treatment begins, the better.

The benefits of early treatment come from avoiding or minimizing the many secondary problems of ADHD. For example, treatment may very well give a person the focus they need to succeed in college—but if they find that focus when they're forty-five, after dropping out of school and suffering through a string of unsatisfying jobs, it's a lot less helpful. It is best when treatment begins in elementary school.

Are there any benefits to ADHD for adults?

For some people, yes. One school of thought holds that the symptoms of ADHD—the impulsivity, the high degree of physical activity, the craving for high-stimulus environments—may actually be an adaptation that helped primitive ancestors survive in a hostile and often-changing world.

Today, we often find adults with ADHD gravitate toward certain professions and lifestyles—for example, the arts. It may be that ADHD makes it easier to make creative leaps between seemingly unrelated concepts, synthesizing them in new ways. Also, certain jobs and lifestyles that offer a great deal of variety and stimulation—daily newspaper reporting or sales, for example—may be especially suitable for a person with ADHD.

Oftentimes people with ADHD will naturally gravitate toward a lifestyle that plays to their strengths. But even artists and freethinkers can benefit from better organizational skills and improved attention, and there's no evidence to suggest that treatments for ADHD diminish creativity or any other beneficial attributes.

I'm a recovering alcoholic, and AA says I shouldn't be taking drugs. Are they right?

As many as a third of people with ADHD have drug or alcohol abuse problems. But ADHD medication doesn't contribute to the problem; in fact, it helps prevent relapses.

Often, substance abuse begins as an effort to self-medicate. Cocaine, for example, seems to have a very different effect on people with ADHD than on those without it. For those with ADHD, it doesn't produce a high so much as create focus.

The problem, of course, is that cocaine is highly addictive. So even though a person with undiagnosed ADHD may start using it to feel normal, the use quickly escalates into dependency.

Or someone with ADHD may start using depressants like marijuana or alcohol—not because it helps her ADHD symptoms, but because it helps blunt the anxiety that often accompanies ADHD.

Stimulants such as Ritalin are chemically related to cocaine, but with an important difference: When they're used *as directed* for ADHD, they aren't addictive. In part that's because the doses are very low.

Also, these drugs don't cause the kinds of psychological changes that you see in drug abuse because of how they work within the brain: They take effect relatively gradually, so they don't produce the "rush" that's associated with a cocaine high. And they wear off the same way, so they don't produce the rapid "crash" and the craving that occurs with cocaine addiction.

As medications such as Ritalin and Dexedrine help resolve the symptoms of ADHD, they can help the user avoid the urge to self-medicate with dangerous and addictive drugs. These medications don't become a *substitute* for addictive drugs; they help resolve the underlying symptoms that led to drug abuse in the first place.

That's not to say that these medications have no abuse potential. They do. That's why a doctor needs to carefully coordinate and monitor treatment for a person with ADHD and a substance abuse disorder. But giving up on medication isn't the solution.

I've followed many of my patients from childhood into adolescence and adulthood, and I've seen how good and timely treatment can unlock their potential. In fact, I've found that working with ADHD patients is the most satisfying work I've ever done, because the results are so profound and positive. With the medical and behavioral tools we now have at our disposal, we can give children with ADHD the gift of a normal life. Once upon a time, they would have been faced with a lifetime of struggle. And worst of all, they'd think it was their own fault—that they were lazy, or stupid, or undisciplined, or simply bad. Now we see them blossom.

I've watched these children grow into remarkable, talented and well-adjusted adults. I've seen families restored. I've seen resentment and conflict replaced by love and joy. It has been a privilege to work with these families and children, and I am honored to count them not only as patients, but as lifelong friends.

CHAPTER 10

How to Find Out More

One of the most important things to remember about dealing with ADHD is that you're not alone. In addition to the support of your school, physician, and other professionals, some of the best help can come from other parents and people with ADHD. Support groups and associations are an invaluable source of information, research, and, most important of all, real-world insights from people who've already dealt with the same challenges you're facing.

Here are key resources:

Attention Deficit Disorder Association (ADDA)
PO Box 488
West Newbury, MA 01985

C.h.A.D.D. (Children and Adults with Attention Deficit Disorder)
499 Northwest 70th Avenue
Plantation, FL 33317
305-587-3700

The leading support group for ADD, with numerous local chapters.

National Coaching Network
PO Box 353
Lafayette Hill, PA 19444

Information resource and forum for ADD coaches.

Orton Dyslexia Society
8600 LaSalle Road
Baltimore, MD 21204-6020
301-296-0232

Focuses primarily on dyslexia, but has taken an active role in issues related to ADHD as well, especially those related to classroom accommodations.

❏ Government Help

Office of Civil Rights
U.S. Department of Education
400 Maryland Avenue, SW
Washington, DC 20202-4135
202-401-3020

The office with primary responsibility for enforcing antidiscrimination rules in public schools.

Equal Employment Opportunity Commission
1801 L Street, NW
Washington, DC 20507
202-663-4900

Resource for help with employment discrimination issues related to ADHD and other disabilities.

Department of Justice
Office of Americans with Disabilities Act
Civil Rights Division

PO Box 66118
Washington, DC 20035

Responsible for issues related to discrimination in places of
public accommodation, including colleges and universities.

☐ Newsletters

The ADHD Report
Guilford Publications
800-365-7006

C.h.A.D.D. ER and
C.h.A.D.D.ER BOX
C.h.A.D.D. National Headquarters
499 Northwest 70th Avenue
Plantation, FL 33317
305-587-3700

Challenge
ADDA
PO Box 448
West Newbury, MA 01985

Rebus Institute Report
1499 Bayshore Boulevard, Suite 146
Burlingame, CA 94010

Good general newsletters.

ADDendum
c/o CPS
5041-A Backlick Road
Annandale, VA 22003

ADDult News
c/o Mary Jane Johnson
ADDult Support Network
2620 Ivy Place
Toledo, OH 43613

Two newsletters for adults with ADHD.

☐ Internet Resources

The World Wide Web has multiple resources about ADHD. Here's a sampling of sites. Web sites change frequently, however. For the most up-to-date listings, use the term "Attention Deficit" in search engines.

- http://ic.net/~msmerza/add/: links to multiple Web sites on ADHD.
- http://www.greatconnect.com/oneaddplace/: A "virtual neighborhood" that serves as a clearinghouse on ADHD information and resources
- http://www.seas.upenn.edu/~mengwong/add/: Archive of information on ADHD.
- http://www.comedserv.com/add.htm: Web site for C.h.A.D.D.

Index